Our
Struggles
are
Real!

Always embrace accountability with others. Love for Both, and yourself.

Rick Crouch

Proverbs 27:17

ISBN 978-1-0980-3944-8 (paperback)
ISBN 978-1-0980-3999-8 (hardcover)
ISBN 978-1-0980-3945-5 (digital)

Copyright © 2020 by Rick Crouch

All rights reserved. No part of this publication may be reproduced, distributed, or transmitted in any form or by any means, including photocopying, recording, or other electronic or mechanical methods without the prior written permission of the publisher. For permission requests, solicit the publisher via the address below.

Christian Faith Publishing, Inc.
832 Park Avenue
Meadville, PA 16335
www.christianfaithpublishing.com

Printed in the United States of America

Thank you, Lisa R. Kline Crouch, you have stood by me through thick and thin, in bad times and worse, you have remained faithful and true. You have been my ever constant, loving, caring and nurturing, the glue that has held our family together. Quite honestly, you are the reason I found myself back in church. Words can neither express my love for you or my remorse for all the pain that I've caused!

Lisa, you are my sunshine, my best friend, my lover and my wife. I love you a bushel and a peck, and a hug around the neck!

> *He who finds a wife finds what is good and receives favor from the Lord.*
> —Proverbs 18:22 (NIV)

> *A wife of noble character who can find? She is worth far more than rubies.*
> —Proverbs 31:10 (NIV)

Contents

Introduction 7
Setting the Stage 11
My Youth 16
Breaking Free 31
Life Together 39
Strained Relationships 53
Outward Appearances 65
Second Chance 77
Near-Death 84
Exposed 88
The Return 94
Preaching Gods Word 104
Twisted and Confused 117
A New Low 132
Casting Stones 142
The Downward Spiral 148
Tarnished 161
Rebuilding 181
Cut Out and Moving On 195
Flat on my Back 203

Rock Bottom Low	216
IronMen	231
Accountability/Discipleship	244
Not Good Enough	258
Going Live	266
A Warrior Stands	280
The Attack	289
Conclusion	309

Introduction

I had joked about writing my life's story for a while now. That is till the day when God really laid it on my heart to "just do it." There are too many men wandering around, feeling like they're alone in a hopeless situation. Their lives are being consumed by their struggles, which is overrun by guilt, fear, and shame.

It is my intent for you, the reader, to connect with me and my life's struggles. Understand that I'm just a common, every day, regular guy; there's no fame or fortune to my story. I've had to get up and go to work every day of the week. Too many times, we have had to scrape by just to survive.

I'm going to be real with you, my stories not pretty. I may have grown up in church, but I didn't know who I was. My identity had many masks; it just depended on the situation and my desires at the time determining

INTRODUCTION

which mask I would wear. I will be open, making myself accountable, transparent in my failures, and ultimately becoming vulnerable to all. There are times that I will repeat myself because there are some points I want to impress into your understanding of who I was and how I felt—the more light from God that I allow to shine in my life exposing the darkness of my selfishness. That has brought me a newfound freedom in Jesus that I have never known before!

If your tired of living a life of secrecy, feeling alone, and defeated. I challenge you to read this book with an open heart and mind. I will talk openly about my struggles with pornography and sexual types of sin until I came to realize it really is an addiction. Statistics don't lie, there are too many people out there struggling—both men and women alike in this rapidly developing age of high-speed technology. Whatever fetish you can imagine is literally at your fingertips.

It's hasn't been an easy journey for my wife and I. It is our desire for you to see there is hope, and that there is a way out. It's our prayers that this book helps you find a shortcut to freedom by learning from my mistakes.

It may not be easy; however, the rewards, well, they're out of this world!

> *Resist him, standing firm in the faith, because you know that the family of believers throughout the world is undergoing the same kind of sufferings.*
> —1 Peter 5:9 (NIV)

Setting the Stage

As men, we don't really like the words, accountability, or transparency. It may be because all we hear in those words is that we have to become vulnerable. And that's not how a man, not a true red-blooded all-American male, responds.

So, why have I come to believe it's important to be in a men's accountability group?

I have learned from my own experiences that we, men, needed to be able to share—if for no other reason than to help relieve the stress in our life. It seems like we would rather keep everything bottled up inside, leading others to believe that we must have it all together. But opening up about our feelings, I'm talking about our honest, down deep feelings, as guys, is *really* hard. When we finally do, we may actually discover that other guys are either facing the same or have faced some of the same issues that we have dealt with.

There is something about women and their make up that enables them to open up and share with other women. But it's different with guys, after all, we're supposed to be big and strong. Oh, from time to time, we can even be a little sensitive—whether it's fear of being seen as week and unable to cope with life issues or our own condemnation and guilt. Men tuck those issues that we battle with away—to perhaps deal with them on our own, another day, maybe.

I grew up in a "Christian" home. And I mean that in the most legalistic and religious way. The way I remember church, it was more a bunch of *don'ts* rather than having a relationship with Christ. Don't make the assumption that my family was locked into and in one church denomination either. It seemed that we had a church circuit—here a while till my parents got upset. Then we would change to someplace else, at least for a while. It just seemed like an unending cycle.

My parents ruled by fear and I was on a very short leash. I didn't have any close friends in my life till I was in high school. As I look back, my relationship with God was much the same way. While God doesn't rule by fear, I had a deep-seated fear of God. I was just a good kid. I think it was fear that kept me from going against my parents. Since I wasn't around any kids my age, other than at school, I had nothing to compare my life with.

There are a few things you need to understand about me and the early years of my life. I was an only child. I was always with my mom and/or my grandparents, which I enjoyed. However, looking back, the love and affection I received from the women in my life were borderline unhealthy. While being an obedient son, even if it was due to fear, I did no wrong. Everything was made about me. As I said, there were no kids close by me outside of school.

Due to my dad's business, most of the other kids' parents didn't like him anyway. Because of those feelings, it seemed to transfer to a dislike of me. It was a classic case of "guilty by association." Kids can be so cruel! Let's just say I was in more than one fistfight because of my last name.

With my mom's sense of paranoia and the fact that I had a lot of issues due to allergies, I wasn't allowed to play baseball or football. I guess because my dad had never played or had much interest in sports, plus the fact that he was gone a lot due to work anyway, it was not a concern to him, and I just went along with it. Yes, I got made fun of at school because of not being in sports. Honestly, I was heavier than the other kids and wore glasses when glasses weren't cool. In all this, I learned to be content in my own little world, after all, that world did revolve around *me*. Since our home was on the same property that my dad's business, a garage, used car lot, wrecker service and salvage yard, was on, I had a lot of places that I could roam, play, and hid.

With the fear of not doing what was right, phrases, such as, "respect your elders," "children are to be seen and not heard," and with the repercussions of disobedience and disrespect, well let's just say the rod was not spared.

> Whoever spares the rod hates their children, but the one who loves their children is careful to discipline them. (Proverbs 13:24, NIV)

Often as my correction, in the form of a spanking, drew near, and I began to pucker up and cry, full of fear of the coming repercussion. I remember hearing words like, "If you want to cry, I can give you something to cry about." Or as my dad would cup his huge hands together, he would say, "Here, cry me a handful."

All these things and so many more contribute to my building wall on the inside—walls that would isolate and protect my emotions, my very being.

We teach our boys at an early age that as a male, they are supposed to be strong, never to show weakness or vulnerability. To be macho and cool, if you cry, well then you're a sissy. Layer upon layer, we construct our walls, guarding our hearts.

As a young boy, there was something inside me, indicating right and wrong. Now I would say it was the Holy Spirit, giving guidance and conviction. Pictures that I shouldn't look at or the fact that I shouldn't take something that didn't belong to me. If I did, I would try to hide it. It's human nature to hide our sin, after all, who likes to get into trouble.

My Youth

Now I did enjoy attending church youth camp—even though the first couple of years didn't start off that way. Maybe it was in part that I was able to get away from home. Even though that in itself was not entirely correct because my parents would always volunteer to help in the kitchen. So it wasn't a total escape. At least the kids at camp accepted me for who I was. Not based on who my parents were.

The dorms were tin buildings with no A/C. Only beds and bunks beds were in the rooms with usually six to eight boys in a room. Of course, the boys' dorms were on one side of the campgrounds with the girls on the other. With the dining hall, snack shack, and commons area separating the two.

The men's restroom and shower area were my nightmare. The tin metal building was divided in three sections—the restroom area, showing area, and the dressing area. None of these areas had any individual partitions. That's right, no privacy at all! The thought of me bearing my nakedness, for others to see me, was a terrifying thought.

The fact was since the afternoon was our recreation time, almost everyone would go down to an open field to play ball. I wasn't a ballplayer, not even as big as I was, I couldn't hit the ball very well. Since my mother helped with lunch, she would go home in the afternoon for about three hours and come back to help with supper. This made it possible for me to go home in the afternoon where I could get a bath and clean clothes. I did this two years before I started showering at camp. Even then, I would get up early and shower first thing in the morning when there was usually no one there.

Rather than facing my fear of my nakedness, my parents had enabled me. They provided a way for me to hide in my shame rather than facing it. I wonder if that's what Adam felt like after eating from the tree of the knowledge of good and evil.

> He answered, "I heard you in the garden, and I was

afraid because I was naked;
so I hid." (Gen. 3:10, NIV)

I was nine years old when I was baptized with my parents. But it was four years later one summer at church youth camp when I actually accepted Jesus into my heart, what a feeling of joy, true life. There was a definite change in my life. I became active in church, excited to attend every service and regularly attended youth group. As opportunity presented itself, I would sing and play my guitar, or even read and share the word of God from behind a pulpit.

I come across the following and decided it would be good to share as it shows my heart back then.

Swearing
Rick Crouch
(A sophomore in Baxter
Springs High School)

So often I hear someone swearing and using God's Name in vain. Every time I hear it, may I use the term, it turns me off. I can't understand how people can down God and His name like they do. God surely is Love, as the scripture bears out in 1 John 4:8.

It is true, the United States Constitution gives us the freedom of speech; but the Bible, of whom God is the author, states clearly that it is wrong to use God's Name in vain and to swear. What God says goes or at least it should go. It is better to obey God than man.

Exodus 20:7 and Duet. 5:11 both read, "Thou shalt not take the name of the Lord thy God in vain: for the Lord will not hold him guiltless that taketh His name in vain." And in Leviticus 19:12 it says, "And ye shall not swear by my name falsely, neither shall thou profane the name of thy God; I am the Lord." By these two scriptures alone, we can tell it is wrong to swear and use God's Name in vain. More scriptures on the subject are: Matthew 5:33-37 "Again, ye have heard that it hath been said by them of old time, Thou shalt not forswear thyself, but shalt perform unto the Lord thine oaths: But I say unto you, Swear not at all; neither by heaven; for it is God's throne: Nor by the earth, for it is his footstool; neither by Jerusalem; for it is the city of the great King. Neither shalt thou swear by thy head, because thou canst not make one hair white or black. But let your communication be, Yea, yea; Nay, nay: for whatsoever is more than these cometh of evil." James 5:12 "But above all things, my brethren, swear not, neither by heaven, neither by the earth, neither by any other oath: but let your yea be yea; and your nay, nay; lest ye fall into condemnation."

Swearing and using God's Name in vain is a sin. In Romans 6:23 it says "For the wages of sin is death; but the gift of God is eternal life through Jesus Christ our Lord."

Think about it. Is it worth the price you must pay for doing it?

Still, there was a battle going on within me. Going to youth camp was like getting a spiritual booster shot of Jesus. Problem was that feeling seemed to only last a couple of weeks. Then the same struggles and the same temptations began to creep back in. Honestly, I didn't know how to handle those feelings. I sure wasn't going to talk to anyone about what was going on in my body, my feelings, and my desires. Besides, who would I even

MY YOUTH

begin to share with? It's so embarrassing! Were these feelings even normal? Am I normal? Why, when I fail, do I feel so much guilt and shame? The thoughts that I've failed, I'm such a failure, seemed to constantly race through my head!

A prime example, when I was a child we had a cookie jar in the kitchen. Our house rule was no cookies before supper. After all, it supposedly ruins your supper. But when there's chocolate chip, my favorite, in that jar—well I had to have at least two. That moment when you get caught leaving the kitchen, with the cookies hid behind your back. It seemed that Mom knew, but if I could just give that innocent look. It was like she didn't know what I had. Ultimately, I was learning the art of secrecy and lying.

Now *as men*, we justify our actions of secrecy. After all, isn't it's safer to keep everything to ourselves? If for no other reason then, simply, if we mess up, no one else knows.

Where is the Accountability?

Where does the Strength come from in that?

Every red-blooded American male, young or old, is going to face a wide range of trails and temptations. And sometimes, we will even get blindsided by them—a true-to-my-life example. You pull on a parking lot, any parking lot really. That's when you notice a young woman, walking across the lot in front of you. Of course, you're supposed to be aware of pedestrians, we don't want to run over anyone. Would you agree that to this point, we've done what we should be doing? It's when the wind blows, causing the woman's skirt to blow open. Oh, my! What do we do with that image? What's our thought? It's so easy to dwell on.

> Therefore confess your sins to each other and pray for each other so that you may be healed. The prayer of a righteous person is powerful and effective. (James 5:16, NIV)

Confess your faults, one to another, yeah right!

That's easier said than done, right? Let's just cut through the chase and stop dancing around the real issue. A proven fact is *all* men, yes even Christian men, struggle with sexual types of sin. In a survey done in 2014, 64 percent of Christian men and 15 percent Christian women viewed pornography at least monthly.

Whether it is pornography or physical lust. It starts in the mind—a thought that pops into our head. We are visual and enjoy those things that are pleasing to our eyes. There is a certain amount of struggles all guys will go through—it's those areas that we can find the greatest pleasures in that we develop addictions!

No, it's not just the lust of promiscuous sex and pornography. But these do rank at the top of the list that *all* men face. We can obsess over literary anything—whether it's the curves of a beautiful woman or the curves of a sporty car. Obsession becomes our idols. All too often, our idols become our addictions. It's not that we intended to fail. We just become wrapped up in the moment. A glance becomes a lingering moment. An acknowledging nod leads to a harmless conversation. One drink leads to, too many.

One thing leads to another with the thought that I'm entitled to a little fun and pleasure. I work hard, I provide for my family. What about my needs, my desires? As we satisfy those feelings once, it becomes easier the next time.

Even as a Christian male, we struggle with how to love our wife like Christ loves the church. How do we handle the emotions of anger to the joy of sex within our marriage and everything in between? There is a lot of issues men face daily—most of which we keep secret.

I can remember when my body started to develop and mature. Life seemed to race on, and my body began to have strange and unsatisfiable urges—whether it was my own misconceptions or the fact that *sex* wasn't ever discussed in my home. Anything relating or pertaining to sex was well just dirty. The things we remember from our childhood. It was in the spring, late afternoon, after school. When my parents decided it was time for "the talk" about the "birds and bees," for some of you that haven't heard that phrase, that's when you explain life, sex and the entire reproduction process to your children. I'll be honest, maybe it was my sheltered life, and I really didn't fully understand sex. It wasn't ever talked about in our home. What I do remember about that talk was my parents stumbling all around the subject. Then my dad got a phone call, and we had to go somewhere. That was the end of that talk, never to be mentioned again.

I remember looking at department store catalog pictures, pictures of adult movie ads that I had collected from the newspaper. Later, I was around twelve years old when I found my first Playboy magazine. As a primal God-given desire, my body seemed to be in a rage that I didn't understand. If sex was in fact dirty, a taboo subject, how was I to understand what's going on inside of me?

I had already discovered masturbating, it would at least bring temporary relief—a moment of pleasure, only to be followed by the feelings of guilt and shame. Another year would roll by, and it was time for church youth camp again. It was a relief, seeing old friends and once again drawing closer to God and realigning my life with Jesus. This time is going to be different! I wanted to live a Godly life, drawing closer to Him in my daily walk.

I had grown up in church my entire life. I heard about God, and I even accept Jesus as my Lord and Savior. But had I really? While I knew that I had experienced a form of Jesus, it just felt like there should be more. Instead, church just seemed like a whole bunch of *don'ts*. Where was God's grace, love, and mercy?

Understand that while some things are unquestionably sin, there can be things in life that you can do that I can't! It's not that anyone has achieved holiness. All too often, I believe "Christians" have a better-than-thou attitude. Or they plead "grace" as a free pass is stumble in sin. Doesn't God want us to rise above, growing closer to Him and to develop a relationship with Him? Do we really comprehend that *we are sons* and *daughters* of God Almighty!

> *And, "I will be a Father to you, and you will be my sons and daughters, says the Lord Almighty."*
> (2 Corinthians 6:18, NIV)

Part of the healing process is to open yourself up, to become transparent, and sharing your personal struggles. Mine was a life of repeated actions—God-believing, repentance, temptation, failure, guilt, ashamed, and frustrated—and *repeat*.

MY YOUTH

My life has always been *very* private. It's the way I grew up, there were some things, like *sex*, you just didn't talk about—not realizing that other guys had the exact same issues, desires, and struggles as me. So I grew up feeling alone, guilty about my actions. I was too ashamed to share my struggles with anyone. Besides, I didn't have anyone who I felt that I could trust enough to share my world of confusion with anyway!

Even though high school, I continued to be active in our youth group, going to Sunday school and church. Only thing was, I still struggled with lust, sexual pressures, and committing the act of self-gratification, as the only means of release that I knew.

Sure I dated, but I was no football jock, I didn't even play. I wasn't exceptionally great looking, but I wasn't a "bad boy." Honestly, I lacked self-confidence, I was just your average guy. Sure when the opportunity arose, I tried to get girls to "sleep" with me, I just didn't have that level of charm or the ability to manipulate and close the deal. And maybe it was God's grace in my life back then that preserved me. I know at the time it didn't feel that way. Truth is, I never had any physical and intimate sexual relations with a girl before I was married—the one thing that forty years ago seemed like a curse. Now seems like it was a blessing—if I had only remained as faithful in my marriage.

It was my senior year on a sunshiny Sunday morning in August. As we walked a half block to where our Sunday school class was going to be, I noticed her walking just ahead of me. A mutual friend said that he thought that she might be interested in going out with me, and if I wanted, he would find out.

How cool it was to have this beautiful, blonde girl from California who was attending her first year of Bible college, interested in me. She was beautiful, smart, sexy, and in the pursuit to know more about God. Our acquaintance developed into strong, deep feelings in a relatively short time. While the Bible college's rules on dating was no solo dates, only double dating was allowed or at least you must have a chaperone. We were good with that, and there was always another couple to double up with or someone just willing to tag along.

Even still, we were able to have some "alone time." Back then, we called it "heavy

MY YOUTH

petting." Yeah, despite the fact that we both were Christians, regardless of the fact she was attending Bible college, I tested the water to see just how far she would let me go, which was not very far at all. I was okay with just kissing, holding her hand or putting my arm around her shoulders. We grew to genuinely know each other, and as our hearts intertwined, we fell in love. This was the one that I could see spending the rest of my life with.

Breaking Free

Something that I haven't shared with you is how controlling my mom really was. As I said, I had dated other girls. There had always come a point, after a month or two of dating the same girl, my dear mother would find some reason that I should stop dating that girl and move on. Since I had always been obedient, as I was ruled with fear, that's what I would do—break up and move on.

Maybe it wasn't me being ruled by, maybe it was just a controlling spirit in my mother. I mean, I get it, I was the only child my parents had. I was my mother's baby boy. In her eyes, there was no girl good enough for me. Strange as it may be, there were things about my mom that I never knew.

It wasn't until years later when she had passed away, and we were going through some boxes, mostly old pictures, I was shocked when I discovered that she had been married not once but twice, and that was before my dad. Sure, I knew Dad had been divorced, even though that was about all I knew. Lisa had picked up on the fact that my dad's ex had been from California. So I'm sure that didn't help matters since Lisa was from California.

Oh, yeah, sure, I had met his daughter, my half-sister, once. But today, I couldn't tell you what she looked like if my life depended on it. That had been one day when I had was with Dad and Mom wasn't with us. I'm not even sure why he had gone by her house; she lived in a small town about twenty miles away.

For me, the ultimate shocker was my mom—the judgmental attitude that she had always had toward people that had been divorced and all the emotions, anger and bitterness that she had locked up deep inside. It must have been like a cancer that eats away at our physical bodies.

Emotions of being ashamed, guilt, secrecy, and the feeling of being unworthy can eat away at our spirit. Left alone, bottled up inside us can only lead to becoming an angry and bitter person. Again, I dare point out my early church experience. There was the hellfire and brimstone if we didn't accept Jesus as your Lord and Savior. Were His love, grace, and mercy?

> But he said to me, "My grace is sufficient for you, for my power is made perfect in weakness." Therefore I will boast all the more gladly about my weaknesses, so that Christ's power may rest on me. (2 Corinthians 12:9, NIV)

Was it possible that all my mother's deep-seated anger and bitterness had robbed her of finding true happiness? To the best of my knowledge, I was her only child, which does explain her possessive attitude, as sick as it seemed. It's only now, years later, even as I am writing this, that I ponder some of these questions.

Like the times before, that point came that my mom decided it was time for me to break it off with Lisa. For me, this time was different. It wasn't like the times or the girls before. It wasn't because we were having sex, like most of my high school friends. "At least most of my friend claimed they were." There was a genuine heart connection with Lisa, God, and I. This time I wasn't the obedient young man; this time, I would pursue love.

Needless to say, the next year was a rough road. Lisa had her schooling and was required to maintain above-average grades. It also included participating in the college choir tour and attending any revival or special services.

Mine was just an average year. I just wanted to graduate, move out of my parents' house, and get married. I had lost any focus on going into the ministry or pursuing any type of schooling after I graduated.

It would seem that my mother had made it her life's mission to break Lisa and I up, by causing problems for Lisa at her college as it was part of our church. Often my Mom would even follow Lisa when she would go into town. There were a lot of false accusations all of which were unsubstantiated. She was focused on Jesus and her studies, maintaining a high-grade point average. Unjustly, Lisa took the majority of the attacks from my mother. The extent of my mother's wrath included calling every board member of the college, voicing her twisted and preconceived ideas. With all the allegations, Lisa developed a strong faith-based prayer life.

While I did get grounded from time to time, I was still able to drive, which meant on the way to and from school Lisa and I could still see each other. And there was our time at church, just to be next to each other, always the stealing of that quick goodbye kiss on Sunday evenings as I walked her to her dorm home.

While I felt God had called me to go into ministry, let me take a moment to share that we are all called to be ministers of God's Word.

> So Christ himself gave the apostles, the prophets, the evangelists, the pastors and teachers, (Ephesians 4:11, NIV)

What I had felt called to was to be a pastor of a church. I was in the town, in a church that was associated with the Bible college. It should have happened! But because of everything that did happen, the embarrassment from my mother, the challenge of keeping our relationship together. We had survived, through time together, as well as time apart. We remained faithful to God and to each other. That's not to say that I didn't still struggle with lustful thoughts. I had just accepted that was normal for a teenage boy and that masturbation was just the mean of release for this inside pressure. I guess there was a part of me that believed that my struggle would magically disappear after I was married.

My focus changed from pursuing God to starting a family. Both are ordained by God, you can do both and be totally in God's will. Both were possible. I just didn't want to press through the pending pressures. It was easier to just graduate, and get a job, a place to live and get married.

Through everything that we faced, everything that we have struggled through, and every adversary, I stand firm that God brought us together, and only by His good grace He has kept us together.

> That is why a man leaves his father and mother and is

> united to his wife, and they
> become one flesh. (Genesis
> 2:24, NIV)

An example of one of those little things that happened that proved it was God, and we were meant to be together. We both had saved money to get married so we began to look at wedding rings. Fortunately for me, Lisa's not into the extravagant type, simple is pleasing for her.

We had looked at a lot of places before we found the rings that we both liked. She had enough to pay for my band; however, rather than taking a chance of the rings being misplaced or lost, we just put everything on layaway together.

It was when I went to pick up the rings that I saw God move. See when we had put her engagement ring, and both her wedding band and mine on layaway, the store had wanted us to just finance the rings. So when I went back in to pick them up, I had planned on financing the balance of $300. It really was more about establishing our credit. After filling out the credit application, they realized that I was only seventeen years old.

They asked if my parents would cosign for us? Yeah, that's not going to happen, I thought. They were going to have to get the finance managers' approval on this. It just so happened that he had gone to lunch. No big deal, we had time to wait for him to get back. It seemed like forever, but he never showed up. Finally, the person that had been helping us went ahead and gave us the rings. They just said to have someone come in and cosign for us.

That was God! We never had a cosigner. In fact, when we made that last payment at the store, the manager made the comment that if we had chosen to not make the payments, there would have been nothing that they could have done because I was a minor at the time of purchase.

Life Together

On January 5, 1980, my beautiful bride walked down the aisle. She had put together a simple but beautiful wedding with the help from a few friends and the $500 her parents had given us for our wedding.

As we stood at the altar, before God, the pastor, and our friends that had gathered together, we were literally holding our breath from fear of my mom causing a scene. We knew prayers were going up for us in our moment. A new chapter was beginning in our life. We didn't have much, but we had God, each other, and a '72 Ford Maverick. I still remember our first night together! Wow! Finally, my life, freedom, and well, my hidden struggles—they were all going to be okay.

Unfortunately, marriage only masked my issues for a season. I had already built my walls without realizing. I was too ashamed to

LIFE TOGETHER

let anyone in, especially the one that I loved so deeply. After all, getting married was going to end my sexual struggles.

Right?

Sadly my coarse of actions eventually continued even during marriage. Don't be mistaken or confused, our married life was good. We enjoyed being with each other in every sense of the word. Lisa was the most caring, compassionate, and a loving woman. I was undoubtedly the luckiest man alive. God had been so good to me.

Bonus, that girl could cook, Mmmm. Even better than my mom! Now she never had cooked for me before we were married. Even though she had said she could cook, I was going on blind faith, and I was truly blessed. If we only had that kind of faith in God.

Yes, we still had issues with my parents, really, it was just my mother. Dad would just go along with her to keep the peace between them, and I understood that!

It really wasn't that long before we decided to start trying, to start a family. After all, it will probably take a couple of months before Lisa would conceive. Maybe longer, right? We had already decided on names for our children while we were dating.

It became evident that our chemistry was quite compatible. Lisa became pregnant within our first month of just trying. Really, it was just that we didn't do anything to prevent it.

We continued to be active in our church. After all, it was the very foundation of our marriage. I had a full-time job, our landlord even cosigned for us to be able to buy a washer and dryer—when we found out we were expecting.

Hurting Lisa, my wife, the one person that *I love*, more than anyone or anything, was the absolute last thing in this world that I wanted to do. Especially with our marriage based on living a Christian life and values. As I look back now, I realize how hypocritical I was trying to live.

True story, even though I'm not sure my wife totally believes this one in its entirety to date, I can't tell you the number of times I have found adult magazines while driving to and from work. I could literally be driving my car at 55 mph and recognizing those glossy pages. Of course, I should stop and pick it up. You wouldn't want it to get in a kid's hands. What an idiot I was to the devil's tricks. Like a kid was going to be driving down the road in a car.

His lies worked, and I continued to struggle. What's wrong with me? I love my wife! I love Jesus! I love my family! I want to make them happy and take care of them, but I'm not really hurting anyone. They're just pictures that I found enjoyment in looking at. I could be alone with a magazine and masturbation, and well, it doesn't hurt anyone. After all, it relieved some of my stress. Even still, I faced the same struggles that I had before marriage.

I know a couple of thoughts going through your mind right about now. Questions like "Didn't your wife want to have sex?" "Didn't you enjoy sex with her?" or "She must not have wanted it as often as you wanted it"—none of which was the case. She enjoyed sex with me. We enjoyed the true intimacy with each other, and it was great! We really did have a great relationship, full trust. We honestly were each other's best friend!

Sure, there was the "not getting any" at times while Lisa was pregnant.

So on March 2, 1981, we officially became parents of our son, Richard. It just seemed like there was something still missing? Maybe it was the fact that our son's needs were now the focus. Life wasn't always just about me anymore.

Maybe in some sick and perverted way, I want to be dominated by a female. After all, my mother had been the dominant one over my life for so long. I really can be reclusive, content in my own world. Possibly because I didn't have many friends growing up, and I learned to play well by myself. In addition, being an only child just made it easier to draw back into my own secrecy. I had no one snooping around to see what I was really doing.

Like I stated, I really did want to provide the best possible life for my family. I've been fortunate to never be without a job for very long. That's not to say that we still didn't struggle to sometimes make ends meet. Lisa and I had decided that we would be dollars ahead if she stayed home with our children. Besides, what kind of values would someone else install in our kids? Since her parents didn't live close by and mine wasn't willing to watch him (and later them), on a regular basis.

To show Lisa's dedication to our little family, we could only afford one car, which I had to have to go to work. Since my job was eighteen miles away in a different town, it didn't make sense for her to take me to work and then come back to pick me up.

We had been renting for a while when we came to the decision that we should buy a home. With the high-interest rates, we came to the conclusion that to buy a mobile home would be our best option. But we still would need a down payment. The big question, where was that money going to come from? With no other option available, Lisa got a job in a clothing manufacturing facility.

Understand my work schedule was Monday–Friday, 5:00 a.m. to 3:30 p.m., and most Saturdays, it would be 5:00 a.m. to 12 noon. Lisa's work schedule was Monday–Friday, 8:00 a.m. to 4:00 p.m.

How can she get to work? And what about our son? We decided we could put him in daycare, just long enough to save the money we needed for a down payment. In order for Lisa to get him to daycare and then get to work, she rode a bicycle with an infant seat, three miles, to drop him off, and then another two and a half miles to work. Then I could pick him up on my way home.

We had survived becoming parents, and now we had our own place. It wasn't much, but despite my secret struggles, it was home! We were happy and blessed.

On December 28, 1983, our daughter, Bethany, was born. which, due to complications, was a small miracle in itself. We had always hoped for a son first and then a daughter next to complete our family. Because of certain issues during the course of Lisa's pregnancy, the doctor strongly advised that she did not go through another pregnancy. So there was a time of rejoicing when it was a girl. I know most young parents find out the baby's sex early in their pregnancy—that's something we never did, maybe it was old school. We just trusted God and waited for the reveal at birth. The one thing that I had always been adamant about was that I would not raise an only child!

Over the next decade, we raised our children in church, attending Sunday school and church every Sunday morning and evening.

And yes, the evening service was even a different message from the morning service. I know it seems that in today's world so many churches have multiple services on the weekend, with the same message repeating.

I remember complaining about having to attend church on Sunday morning, again that evening, and yet again on Wednesday evening. Now as I truly hunger for more of God. I miss not having those opportunities.

Yet, if we look around, we may discover we have opportunities, just in a different form or ways that the body of Christ can come together and grow. Maybe we can have a life or cell group, a men's or women's discipleship or accountability group, women's missionary group, Bible studies, or being able to serve those less fortunate. Why did I just single out women for missionary groups? All are called to share the gospel.

Guess what, we grew up hearing how important it is to be active in your youth group. What makes us believe that it stops there, in just our youth? As adults, we have acquired more issues than our youth ever thought of. This alone would lead me to believe we need to continue being active in some type of group.

Over those ten years, there was a slipping away that was slowly happening. Both Lisa and I had taught Sunday school classes at one time or another. We at least had a decent understanding of the word of God. I just wanted something more since life had become such a routine. The monotony of working Monday through Saturday at noon and then followed by church on Sundays. Maybe church had just become going through the motions. Getting up on Sunday morning, dressing in our Sunday best, which back then we either wore a suit or dress slacks, dress shirt and tie, and what was generally the most uncomfortable dress shoes. Then we would go to a building that we called the church, pretending to be someone we're not, singing the same old hymns, the preacher talking about something and closing with a prayer, only to repeat the same cycle the next service, the next week, the next month, etc.

I could play the game well, there was the me at church, the me at home, and then there was the secret me. The magazines that I found and the ones I did actually purchase offered a fantasy. The women that would cater to my every desire. They would do anything and everything that I could imagine to bring me the pleasure that I deserved. And nobody needed to know, as it was my world, and the girls in the pages, well they would never tell.

There's something that you need to understand. Maybe it was from the fear that I had grown up with. Then again maybe it was the conviction of the Holy Spirit. But every foul, perverse, lustful, deceitful thing I ever did, I did with the fear of getting caught, a fear of being exposed, a fear of losing my wife, and my family! It was a dark, driving force that drove my actions. I had thoughts like, I work hard, I provide a good life for my family, and I deserve a little pleasure. After *all* that I do, I'm not hurting anyone, and besides, I'm entitled. Can you begin to see what I couldn't see for all those years? All my actions revolved around me and my *selfishness*.

Still, after every act, I faced guilt, shame, self-condemnation, remorse, feelings of unworthiness, failure, and being one big failure. Despite all those thoughts, as intense as they were at times, I continued down the same path that I was on. For a while, I would offer up my token repentance to God, which eventually even that would change. My life and my actions were still a big secret, after all, it was *my* life.

For some reason, it never was quite enough. What started years ago, looking at the girls in swimsuits and bras, in department store catalogs. Evolving to playboy magazines, to the more hardcore XXX adult magazines, never finding satisfaction. Seeking some kind of fulfillment as I continued to spiral out of control, next was phone sex lines. Actually believing that they wanted to talk with me, telling me all the things that I wanted to hear. So what if most of them were cheesy recordings? The fact that one of the numbers was 1-800-XXX-LISA, I could just claim that it was my Lisa. It wasn't like I was actually talking with another woman.

Understand that my struggle wasn't an everyday event. It could be a day, a week, or even sometimes going a month or two between my incidents. The talk lines were lame, and there were charges anyway. It wasn't long till I convinced Lisa, while that's not exactly true, I brought it up and being the "good/submissive" wife, and she went along with me. So with that, we started watching "adult movies." After all, it will help enhance our sex life and spice things up a bit. After all, Lisa and I was watching them together!

She seemed okay with it, as long as she was there. Sure, she didn't like it if I was looking at a magazine or watched a movie when she wasn't there. I'm not sure why it really mattered if she was there or not. I knew that I wasn't about to let her see my private hardcore magazines. I didn't want to "hurt" her in that way, I guess deep down I knew how degrading they were to women. By me not sharing those dark, and twisted, secret desires, in my mind I was "protecting" her.

I had learned earlier that wording was everything. After all, my dad was quite possibly one of the best salesmen ever. And a half-truth isn't a lie. There was no need for people to know everything. If you play your wording right, you can tell anyone what they want to hear, even some of what they don't and they'll never even catch it.

In all honesty, I *never ever* wanted to hurt Lisa. In my heart, down deep, I have *always loved her*! No matter what I had done, it didn't matter what lies I told. I didn't relate any of that to hurting her. I would stand on sections of scripture—like wives submitting to their husbands. With the attitude of that, she had to be mindful of what I wanted. It was a scripture that will keep the women in their place. Let's look at that scripture in its entirety:

> For the husband is the head of the wife as Christ is the head of the church, his body, of which he is the Savior. Now as the church submits to Christ, so also wives should submit to their husbands in everything. Husbands, love your wives, just as Christ loved the church and gave himself up for her to make her holy, cleansing her by the washing with water through the word. (Ephesians 5:23–26, NIV)

See how we can twist God's word? I only wanted to use "wives should submit to their husband," as a means of getting the desired result that served me and my agenda. Maybe in my own unhealthy way, I was loving and protecting her. But wasn't that protecting just of my own secrecy, using God's word to manipulate? I sure wasn't living up to my part and loving her the way Christ loves us.

From department store catalogs, pornographic magazines, phone sex lines, Adult movies, and chat rooms—my addiction only spiraled more out of control. I could justify anything. After all. having phone sex isn't cheating on my wife. There wasn't any physical sexual relations with another woman. So I'm not breaking that marriage commitment. However, the further I went, it was never enough. It was like a drug. I want to find that perfect high of the ultimate sexual encounter.

Strained Relationships

In the first ten years of marriage, we had two children, bought our first home, and now we had two vehicles. Sure, we had our struggles as any young couple does—all the while I still secretly struggled with my obsession with pornography. Keep in mind it wasn't a huge daily battle, it wasn't even something that I spent much money on. However, the fact that I was a selfish and self-centered person, the issue that things had to go my way had become evident to Lisa.

It saddens me to look back at that time of our life. It was the best of times, and it was the worst of times. Anyone else with a different personality most certainly would have left me. And rightfully so, I hadn't lived up to those scared vows of marriage! "To love, cherish, honor and respect.

Even still, from time to time, we tried to make amends with my parents. It never seemed to last for very long. The way we chose to live our life, never quite measured up to them. I remember we had them over for supper. In case, you don't remember me saying it, Lisa was/is a fantastic cook.

Anyway, Mom was helping out in the kitchen. There was something they needed out of the refrigerator. No big deal, Mom went to get it. As she opened the door, she saw my twelve-pack of beer. The kicker was her response as it wasn't even directed at me. I wasn't trying to hide it. I had given up on living my life to try to please them. I expected Mom to perhaps point out that I wasn't raised that way, drinking, and that I know better, or what would God do? I was geared toward any number of religious responses she might say. Except for the one thing, she asked Lisa as she closed the refrigerator door, "What have you done to my son?" She had turned my actions into something to do with Lisa even when Lisa had nothing to do with the beer in the first place.

While we maintained a strained relationship at best with my parents, we would visit every weekend. That would maybe last for a month, no more than three months. I would get fed up with the little jabs at Lisa and their constantly trying to tell us how to run our life, how to raise our kids, and how we should or shouldn't spend our money. As they were always telling us what we should do, then whatever we did, well, that was wrong too. When I had enough of my parents' attitude, we just wouldn't go around for a while. My philosophy was, it's the same distance from our home to theirs as it was from their home to ours.

It was *always* Lisa that would encourage me that we should go visit them—especially since her parents lived so far away, and the kids should be around at least one set of grandparents. It was just another vicious and unsuccessful cycle in our life.

We knew several couples that were around our age. They would share about how their folks helped them out in tight situations. One couple shared how his parents had even given them the down payment for a home. It's not like we expected my parents to financially support us, but their support, of any kind, would have been appreciated.

I was working ten-hour days and seven hours on Saturday and six hours on Sunday's from time to time. I was providing my family with a good life. We had everything that we needed and some things we just wanted. We were going to make it on our own, and besides, if we were going to make it, we didn't have a choice. It would have to be on our own.

There are three sections of my story that is extremely hard for me to share about. However, if I'm writing this, trying to convey the importance of men becoming open and honest, that freedom from addiction, specifically in my case pornography, is possible! By using words like "accountability," "transparency," and "becoming vulnerable," I have no other choice but to continue on. This is the first of those three occasions.

The economy took a nosedive, work slowed down, and my hours were cut. The positive I still had a job and was still putting in forty hours a week. The downfall was the loss of my overtime—that hurt the pocketbook. Without realizing it, we had grown accustomed to a paycheck with that extra income not being so extra anymore. Now, what are we going to do? My parents wouldn't help, even though they were financially able. We also knew Lisa's parents would help equally, and we also realized that they weren't setting in a financial position themselves to help us out, even if they wanted.

Lisa had picked up some house cleaning jobs. That way, she could work around our kids' school schedule. Still, that just wasn't enough. Eventually, there was no other option, but bankruptcy.

This was hard for me to accept, I had been taught and firmly believed in working hard, paying your bills, and owning up to your responsibilities. Those that didn't were low life, deadbeats. This was literally against everything that I had grown up believing about life and finances. What kind of man had I become? We had lost our home and a car. The embarrassment, it was personally humiliating. Maybe it was just my own feelings of being a failure. I was angry, mad at myself for letting my family down. I questioned if, in some aspects of our life, my parents had been right in those areas.

No, the one thing that I fully believed and never doubted was that Lisa and I were meant to be together. Still, I had let her down. The guilt and shame from that alone hurt. We didn't tell anyone unless it was absolutely necessary!

Granted, there was some good that came out of that mess. See, we were living in my hometown, where everybody knew everyone's business. Because of my father's business, most people didn't really care for my family. Again, years later it was still guilty by association. I'd like to think that I'm nothing like my father. Actually, I've been told that I'm not like him, still, people's words can hurt.

I remember one time when Lisa was helping with one of our sons' class's parties in grade school. The commit was made, "How did someone like you get mixed up with a family like that?"

So, we moved eighteen miles away, which only made sense as that's where I worked anyway. In a way, it was a new beginning. As our new journey started we began to rebuild our life and our credit, my struggles continued. I was increasingly curious about what it would be like (sexually) to be with someone else. As I watch adult movies, the excitement, the long-lasting pleasures, multiple partners, women eager to satisfy their partners ever desire. In a world seemingly free of all conflict and stress.

I knew the Bible verse:

> But I tell you that anyone who looks at a woman lustfully has already committed adultery with her in his heart. (Matthew 5:28, NIV)

So if I'm going to look, I may as well enjoy the act. I mean, let's be honest here, if I've already sinned by looking, it's not going to make any more difference in physically doing the act, right? Besides, the commit had been made that extramarital affairs can create stronger marriages. It wasn't that our marriage was bad. Just in my eyes, some of the spark was gone.

It was my way of thinking and my selfishness that lead to a number of arguments with Lisa. I still loved her, very much so. I just wanted her to be more adventurous, more outgoing. If she wasn't going to be, I was sure I could find someone who would be.

I become more chatty in conversations with women. Being complementary to them, telling them the things that they might like to hear. Most of the women where I worked had a reputation anyway. Finally, one day, after having multiple conversations with a certain gal, as she was about to walk away, she smiled and wrote her name and number on a piece of paper. Which she dropped it in the top of my toolbox. A number of thoughts went through my head, finally, the possibility of adventure.

There was something in my heart, I still loved Lisa. I was scared, what if the experience was lousy? What if others found out? What if I got some strange diseases? How would I explain that? No, I couldn't do that as much as a part of me really wanted to. But with fear gripping me, I knew that I just couldn't go through with it.

It was a few months later, Lisa and I were invited to go dancing with four other couples from work. I had started drinking, more socially than anything. Besides, having an occasional beer or two has actually been found to be healthy for a person. Right?

OUR STRUGGLES ARE REAL!

It was a fun and relaxing evening as we all danced, laughed, and had a few drinks. As I danced with another man's wife and my wife danced with her husband, the perverse and lustful thoughts ran ramped in my mind. In fact, my thoughts must have been heard by my dance partner. At the start of that dance, there had been two sets of boundaries laid out. Lisa quickly established a distance between him and her, which was respectful and safe. Myself, on the other hand, had continued with my flirtation. As the song ended and a slow song began, I found her body pressing against mine. The way her leg rubbed against me, as we slowly moved to the slow music, it was in the gentle way that she lead our bodies to sway with the music. I understood her intentions. I was no longer the pursuer, rather the pursued. I felt like a fly in a spider's web even though it was this type of situation I had thought that I wanted.

As Lisa and I drove home that night, we discussed and laughed about the situation that I had got myself into. How that maybe I should learn a lesson from the evening and move on. I can't help believing that once again I was a disappointment to Lisa that night. Because of things that had happened in her family. Lisa had seen what that type of behavior does to a marriage. How it invades and causes hurt and heartache, ripping a family apart. She had cared enough about me and our relationship to establish boundaries—when all I did was push the boundaries.

In a way, it did teach me a few things. To be content in my secret world, the one with the women that would do anything I wanted. I would live out my fantasies through the acts the women did while I watched the occasional adult movie. I would fantasize about any woman that I saw who was dressed in a provocative way, peeking my lustful desires. After all, I was sure they wanted to be noticed in a sexual way. There, in my mind, they all would do what they were told to do and they would like it, begging for more.

With these thoughts and images impressed deep within my mind. All I needed was a few minutes while taking a *hot* shower, there I would achieve the release my body craved.

Scriptures like Matthew 5:28 didn't understand the needs of my manhood!

OUR STRUGGLES ARE REAL!

Our life together did seem somewhat better after that night out. We began to work on getting some of that old spark back in our marriage. I still had my secret desires, that no one needed to know about. In the course of reestablishing our credit, we had bought Lisa a car. And since both the kids were in school, she got a full-time job—that's in addition to her full-time job of homemaking. From the very beginning of our marriage, she has taken care of virtually all the domestic responsibilities of our home. I'm not claiming to do much around the house. I do from time to time make a conscious attempt to help. I still don't understand completely the method to her madness. I just appreciate, not only the cleanliness of our home but the way she takes care of our things. With her working, the plan was to save enough money to buy a house. There was still a certain level of her not really sure about trusting me—as a way to show my love for her. One day, that I was off and she had to work. I got a heart with her name tattooed on my right forearm. I remember getting home only after she had already been home for a while. Her first question was, "Where had I been?" I heard the doubting of my loyalty in her voice. Here's where I've been as I revealed my arm.

I had become more open with my fleshly hunger for worldly pleasures and desires. Some of which I had persuaded Lisa to compromise her values for—tactics of abusing her mentally, questioning her value as a woman or wife, questioning her willingness or lack thereof, to take care of her man, in the manner that *I wanted* my desires met. After all, her needs weren't "that" important.

I still had my secrets, my fantasies, and my time to relieve the insurmountable pressure myself. It didn't matter, I could masturbate, gratifying myself in the early evening. Later that same night, I would have sex with my wife as if nothing happened. Yes, in my mind, our marriage was headed in the right direction—despite my selfishness and my acts of secrecy.

Outward Appearances

While my focus of writing this has been on my life's struggles, maybe I should back up a moment to explain myself and who I am in my development of what we call life. I've always been just average and I don't believe I've ever really excelled at anything. Scholastically, my grades were on average Bs and Cs. The fact was nothing just came easy, and I had to work at it to keep my grades up. In fact, sometime around the fifth grade, I had to have a tutor. I hated English, thank goodness for extra credit book reports.

While I was in elementary school, I suffered from allergies. My parents, being who they were, overly cautious and protective, took me to a specialist where they tested me for what seemed like everything under the sun. It was these little inch-round circles with an injection of, we'll say potato, it could be chocolate, house dust, dog or cat hair, the list is seemingly endless, in the center of the circle. If that area turned red, possibly whelping up that indicated an allergic reaction, depending on how red and how swelled it was indicated the severity of allergy to, in this case, potato.

I had countless visits as they continue to do, probably forty or fifty at a time on my back. To a boy, in the third grade, it seemed that I was allergic to everything—grass, cat hair, dog hair, chocolate, and house dust. Anything fun or that tasted good, but those are the ones I remember the most. Because of that, my parents limited my activities. No sports like little league baseball or football were in my future.

I believe it was around sixth grade that I tried band and the trombone. Yeah, that didn't last long. Next thing I remember, it was probably during junior high, my parents let me take guitar lessons. Maybe it was in part because they didn't let me do the baseball or football thing. I never even went just to watch any of the games, at least until I started driving. The guitar, it was okay. I learned enough to occasionally sing and play at church. I knew the basic chords, but honestly, I didn't have the finger coronation.

My dad literally worked all the time. Even when we went on vacation or even went anywhere for that matter, he was doing something work-related. I suppose that's part of owning your own business. He had never cared for sports, not even hunting or fishing. Now my grandfather, back in his day, would hunt and fish. However, he was involved in a mining accident, which left one of his legs shattered. So that ended his hunting and his fishing was limited. I can remember going with him and my mom twice. Once was a pond the other a river.

It was in junior high that I was able to try out for wrestling. That was my one sport, that I participated in my two years of junior high and all four years of high school.

I was tall and lanky, and my freshman year was, to say the least, challenging. Time and again, I would get pinned. But each match, it would take my opponent a little longer to win. Sure, I won a few matches, but the greater accomplishment was my determination to not get pinned.

There was one particular guy that had beat me early in the season. I had given him a good run, but according to his teammates, he had been sick. We faced off again in the last match of the regular season. Word was, he was healthy and had a point to prove. He attacked with a vengeance, and while most of that match, I spent on my back. That night, I may have lost, but that Titan didn't get the pin.

Later on in life, I had a friend that took me fishing. After catching one fish, I was hooked, as I really did enjoy it. I never became obsessed with just "having to go." Sure, I bought the equipment, and I even bought a twelve-foot flat bottom boat and trolling motor, which was more than enough boat to go fishing where we went. When my son got old enough, I started taking him. That's when I learned to swim.

Lisa had stepped in and said if I was taking him fishing, then we both needed to learn to swim. And she was right. If we were going to be on the water, it was only smart. I had taken swimming lessons back when I was a kid, that had been a joke. I could walk across the pool as well as I could swim across, at least where they were having us swim. I was actually glad that I was going to be gone on the last day of class because for our final swimming test, we were going to have to jump off the high dive board. There was absolutely *no way* I was going to do that. It looked way too scary for me, besides I knew that I couldn't swim in deep water. But twenty years later, I learned to swim and you know what, it's fun.

It's sad to say but I don't remember ever spending that much quality time with my dad. It was only after I had my driver's license that I went with him to pick up a car and that was work related for him. There was one time that I helped rebuild a motor, another time I helped pull a motor and put it in a car that we were fixing for me to drive. The car was a 1971 Chevy Monte Carlo—she was nothing fancy, but man she would run. I may or may have not buried that speedometer on more than one occasion—it's 120 mph if you're wondering what the speedometer would register.

Later, Dad and I rebuilt a motor for a truck I was restoring. I had gone with him enough to know how to operate a wrecker. All that stuff was relatively simple and good to know. There just wasn't what I would call a true relationship with him. It was always about working, providing for his family and how he could turn a buck to make more money. That's what I remember about my dad.

I suppose that I learned self-reliance—is that always a good thing, to not be dependent on anyone? I think perhaps it's a double-edged sword. Spiritually, Scripture tells us to lean not on our own understanding. Physically/financially, growing up, we learn that we should stand on our own two feet. To not rely on or trust anyone.

If we indeed learn to stand on our own, does that make it harder to ask for help? I know pride can come into play also. Understanding that Jesus told us to ask for anything—granted whatever you ask for must be in line with God's will and His word.

Can you see where I'm going with this? Growing up, we are so focused on the physical then later on when we come to Christ. Believing in the spiritual, we often struggle to grasp this whole new concept of putting faith in and trusting God. That there is so much more to life then just monetary means.

As a parent, I failed in so many different ways. I was so wrapped up in my selfish desires, and Christ wasn't my focus. Dads (and moms) need to spend time in prayer with our children. Let them hear our prayers as we stand in the gap for them and others, praying for a hedge of protection around our family. We should be speaking blessings and direction in their lives—physical, spiritual, mental and emotional.

As I take advantage of every opportunity to pray with my granddaughters, I can begin to see how impactful it is in their life, how it begins to shape their values and build their faith, and also developing a reliance on God.

Whether you want to call it cheap, poor, thrifty, tight, smart, or economical when something needed to be done or fixed, I did it myself. From water literally pouring from under our home due to a broken line, roofing a house, building a shed, making picture frames, tiling a floor, and even making furniture for our home. From appliances to automotive, I would at least attempt to do it myself.

One-piece I'm extremely proud of is a cradle that I built. I built it to be a legacy piece to be passed along to our kids as they had kids. To date, each of our four grandchildren did time in it. Their names and birth dates are on the bottom. I hope one day that cradle has my great, great-grandchild in it.

I remember when our kids were little and our washing machine broke down. While taking a look at it, I discovered the belt had broke. Easy fix, right? The next day after work, I went by and picked up a belt. Now I didn't have a diagram showing how the belt was laced or anything. That was before you could just Google everything. It should be easy enough, and I had changed the serpentine belt on a car before.

Know I've never been a violent person. However, Lisa had come to understand that when I'm having a difficult time with something I'm working on. It's just best to leave me alone!

It was a Wednesday evening, and we had planned on going to church. However, getting the new belt on was giving me fits. When I came back in the house with a crowbar, Lisa decided it was time to take the kids and go ahead and go to church. All I'm going to say, is when they got back that evening, the washer was working.

I fit the phrase, "Jack of all trades, master of none," even though in the forty years since high school, I've only held five full-time jobs. When I graduated, I was working at a small independently owned grocery store, because of my personality and customer service. I was offered a job in a meat market. There, I learned the skills of a butcher. As two companies merging together often has downfalls, I left there for a job making more money, going into restaurant management. As it turned out that place wasn't fairing much better. It was in a last attempt to turn things around before closing their doors. I had always enjoyed working with people. Up to this point, everything I had done involved some type of customer service, interacting with people.

I had a family now, more responsibilities, which meant that I needed a stable job. For the next seventeen years, I worked in a machine shop. The pay wasn't bad, and when business was good, there was always overtime. After years of faithful service, hard work, and seldom ever missing a day, you would think that I would be considered for a promotion. It was discouraging to never have the opportunity to advance or "moving up" in the company.

I took a new job and a pay raise going to a manufacturing plant. Sure, I've had several side jobs. In addition to my full-time jobs, picking up some extra cash is always good. I even tried to get a small handyman business for myself going. But that's really tough if you don't have the right people to help you.

We allowed our kids to at least try any extra school activities they wanted. As I look back, perhaps we should have been more demanding in their participation. While it wasn't school-related, our son, Richard, was active in cub scouts advancing into boy scouts as he got older, which lead the way for Lisa and me to become active in scout leadership. High school sports never was Richard's thing. Band, marching band, choir, and show choir was what he loved doing.

While our daughter, Bethany, tried the girl scouts. But because we had been so active in boy scouts, there had been a lot of times when she was drug along. She had already picked up on things like the different knots and camping. In our area, boy scouts are more active than the girls. So after joining the girl scouts as a Brownie, Bethany was a little disappointed. She had no desire to join for a second year and we weren't going to force her.

In middle school, Bethany had the height and went out for basketball—until one of her coaches was cussing the girls out. At which point she informed them that nobody talks that way to her at home and she's not going to be talked to that way at school. Sad moment and proud moment!

It was Bethany that picked up a guitar. For a while, she even played in the youth praise band. Fact is, she is currently on her churches Praise and Worship Team.

In our mid-thirties, we were on the health kick and working out four to five times a week. By that time, we had dropped out of church altogether. We created a different temple in our physical body. Myself, being tall has its advantages, but there are disadvantages as well. It's really tough to add muscle mass to a six-foot-five-inch frame.

We were just too busy with our life. Besides, the gym provided plenty of eye candy for me to feed my flesh on.

In our mid-forties, after our kids were out of the house, I laid the weights down, bought a motorcycle, and began doing curls, twelve ounces at a time. For about ten years, Lisa and I had a small group of friends that rode and partied together. Our vacations were road trips. seeing the country on two wheels. Going to bike rallies and bars always proved to be a good time. You never knew what you might see. Again, it was just another way that I could feed my fleshly desires.

Lisa has remained a faithful friend and trusted wife through every twist and turn that I've made. Now I've introduced you to my outward appearance and my family.

Second Chance

It wasn't long till we began the process of trying to buy a house. We had reestablished our credit the best we could. Now we were just going to have to wait and see what happens.

Having gotten away from God, I'm not even sure we prayed about being able to buy a home. Really, I'm not sure we prayed about anything anymore. As I look back to that time, we were just going through the motions of life, raising and providing our kids with what we considered a good life while seeking any pleasure life might offer along the way.

It wasn't long till we were approved to purchase a brand new home—nothing that was big and fancy, that wasn't who we were anyway. It sure wasn't Lisa. She has never been about the fancy, rather the simple and what's practical. Myself, I have to be cautious. With thoughts like "Bigger/newer real is better!" I mean that was my dad's attitude, which unfortunately I can have a tendency to gravitate in that direction.

Our new home would suit our family and our needs. It was good to know that we were about to have a house that was going to be our home! It gave me a certain sense of self-worth, a major accomplishment!

It does sadden my heart to know that *we* didn't recognize that as a blessing from God. But does God allow blessing in our life despite the way we live our lives?

> We pray this so that the name of our Lord Jesus may be glorified in you, and you in him, according to the grace of our God and the Lord Jesus Christ. (2 Thessalonians 1:12, NIV)

Let's read that in the Common English Version.

> Then, because of the undeserved grace of God and our Lord Jesus Christ, you will

> bring honor to the name of our Lord Jesus, and he will bring honor to you. (2 Thessalonians 1:12, CEV)

I like that, "the undeserved grace of God and our Lord Jesus Christ!" We lived undeserving for so many years. I know that back then, I wasn't bringing any honor to Him. But my desire is to give Him *all* honor and glory, now! As I write this, I find myself reflecting back, realizing how often God was there, waiting for, and wanting me, to *wake up*!

> I pray that the eyes of your heart may be enlightened in order that you may know the hope to which he has called you, the riches of his glorious inheritance in his holy people, (Ephesians 1:18, NIV)

All I could see was my family, my desires, and my pleasures, whatever would give me the greatest pleasure, satisfaction and fulfillment.

It was exciting that as we had purchased our home while it was under construction. We had choices to make like what color of shingles, the color of the brick and siding, the carpet, the color of the walls, ceilings fans, and light fixtures to pick out. There were moments of confusion, numerous long and busy weekends; and side-by-side, we were building memories. Ultimately, life was good, it felt like we were finally headed in the right direction in our life together.

There were a lot of things that we wanted to do around our new house. True, the house itself was the way we wanted, but the property needed work, it was a blank canvas. We spent one whole weekend tilling up the entire yard and doing our landscaping from scratch. There were flowerbeds to design and Lisa wanted a rose garden. We put up a privacy fence around the backyard and made an area for a small vegetable garden. It was cheaper for me to build a storage shed compared to buying one. We were busy for the first year just getting things shaped up like we wanted them.

With a new home, kids in middle school, and all that comes with life also came a desire for more stuff. I was making a decent wage, the economy had picked up, which meant overtime at work. I had been at my job for seventeen years with no advancement. My attendance was perfect or near-perfect, year after year. I was doing the same thing repeatedly year in, year out. I was becoming bored with my job.

Several of the guys I had worked with had gotten on at a plant across town. It was swing shift work, but their starting pay was more than I was making after all the years I had put in where I was at. Lisa and I talked about it and agreed it would be worth checking out.

Since I knew a guy that worked for that company, I reached out to him. It would seem that my resume was seen by all the right people. It wasn't long before I had an interview, and I was going to be changing jobs.

I was making more money than I ever had in my life. The first two to three months were great as somehow, I was lucky enough to get put on straight days, Monday through Friday. Sure, the hours were long but that wasn't an issue. When my luck ran out, I was put on the line, which the plant run production twenty-four-seven—for those that may not understand that's twenty-four hours a day, seven days a week. The way you were scheduled, you worked twelve-hour shifts, swinging from days to nights. Generally, three days in one week and four days the next week. It seemed that they always needed extra help, so you could easily pick up an extra day on your three-day/thirty-six-hour week.

Even though I worked long and hard hours, I had more time off. While it sounded great, like everything there was negative drawbacks. More often than not, my time off was when Lisa and the kids were gone, which gave me time to get things around the house done.

While we had been pouring our heart into turning our house turning it into a home, creating our own haven. I didn't seem to have the sexual struggles. Then again maybe I was just too tired or had I become desensitized to what was morally wrong. Maybe it was time in the gym that helped me take my focus in a different direction.

Even though we had been regularly working out for several years at that time, however, even in the gym, I could feed my flesh. It wasn't a dungeon full of sweaty guys, gals worked out too. And they wore tight little outfits. Plus Lisa worked out and, we both were in good physical shape.

My reasoning for sharing this is to simply reinforce the fact that my wife was/is very much an attractive and desirable woman herself. Always in support of me, doing more than the normal wife would. Life was good! After all, I was getting my way.

Near-Death

It was 1995 Christmas break and Bethany, our daughter, had a friend over, for a sleepover. It was in celebration of Bethany's twelfth birthday. Even though her birthday was only three days after Christmas, we have always kept them separate.

Richard and I were at the gym working out when my wife called. Bethany had laid down to take a nap. When Lisa tried to get her up, she was groggy and incoherent, her skin was pale and clammy. Lisa had managed to get her to the car and was taking her to the hospital emergency room.

As we got there, of course, Lisa was upset, but there was a sense of turmoil. Evidently, during the check-in process, a nurse had accused Lisa of giving Bethany a drug overdose. They had attempted to do a spinal tap and one nurse had thrown a tray across the room as she thought that she had stuck herself with a needle. There had already been at least a half dozen cases that fall/winter of kids getting bacterial meningitis. CDC; Centers for Disease Control and Prevention was on full alart and to date, none had survived, so yeah, the tension was at a high level.

As Bethany's pediatric doctor arrived, she calmly and successfully did the spinal tap herself. Not even waiting for the test results, the doctor made arrangements to Med flight Bethany to a larger hospital sixty miles away. They were better equipped to handle what did appear to be the life-killing disease that had been so active that year.

As our daughter was flown away, we quickly rushed home, gathered a few essential items and drove ourselves to where our daughter was, really with little to *no* hope of ever seeing her alive again.

Upon our arrival, they confirmed it was, in fact, bacterial meningitis. Bethany had to be quarantined, in a tent and in ICU. Only one person could go in her room at a time, and they had to dress out in full scrubs and a mask.

Fortunately, the hospital had an area for families of patients in critical condition. This allowed us a bed to at least try to sleep and get a shower, so we didn't even have to leave the hospital.

Lisa's mom and sister flew in from California to be a support. It was such a stressful time that Lisa ended up with severe stress headaches. We were really lucky that she didn't end up in the hospital herself.

I'm ashamed to say I really wasn't much support to anyone. I was angry with the fact that I may lose my little princess. I allowed the anger to fuel my selfishness, failing to turn to God. After all, a "loving God" wouldn't allow an innocent child to suffer. It was a long week, to say the least—despite the fact that we had been given little hope, there was a gradual improvement.

Soon, we were able to bring our baby girl home. There was still home health care that was needed, but she had beat the odds. That season, there were eleven deaths with only three survivors of bacterial meningitis. We were so thankful that our daughter was one of those survivors.

Now you would think that after an experience like that, a person, a family would turn to God! Seriously, how blind does a person have to be? Bethany's recovery was nothing short of a miracle. This was orchestrated by a God, designed to be a testament of His goodness and grace.

Calloused by my selfish desires, I continued to serve myself.

Exposed

As I began working swing shift, I had to learn to sleep during the days. With the kids at school and Lisa often at work, the house was quiet enough. Too quiet! Over the years, I thought that I had to have sex to relax in order to go to sleep.

I had taken something so beautiful, created by God Himself for a purpose as well as our pleasure, turning it into an obligation for Lisa. It was something she was afraid not to do for fear of what I might do if she didn't give me sex, and meet my desires. Our sex was losing the intimacy that connects a husband and wife's soul. It was becoming more of an obligation for Lisa instead of a time of bonding and true intimate unity.

How was I going to be able to get to sleep? Just looking at pornographic pictures wasn't satisfying the rage inside anymore.

OUR STRUGGLES ARE REAL!

Maybe just a phone call to one of the many numbers in the back of the magazines. It says it's a real, live girl, and she'll do anything I want—*no* credit card needed!

I attempted to go through with the call on several occasions. I just listened to the sexy seductive voice that introduced their service. Then one day, I pressed #1 and entered a "chat room." It wasn't at all what I expected or even wanted. There was actually more thrill in just listening to the sexy seductive voice on the introduction of the variety of services that I can choose from. My whole experience with this adventure had been a huge letdown. I did find the pleasure that I needed to "get off" while listening to their seductive voice even if I could tell they were prerecorded. It was my little secret, no one, not even Lisa had even a hint.

> But if you fail to do this, you will be sinning against the Lord; and you may be sure that your sin will find you out. (Num. 32:23, NIV)

EXPOSED

It was just a normal day at work when I was told that I had a phone call. As I answered, my mind was racing, not knowing what could possibly be wrong. It was Lisa, words can't express the hurt that I heard in her voice and how upset and disgusted she was. She told me the phone bill had come in the mail and that there was an unexplained charge on our bill. Curiosity had gotten the best of her, so she had called to find out what the charge was for. What had I done? Did I make the call to a phone sex line?

In a panic of fear, I did the only thing I knew to do, *lie*! It had worked before. I just had to spin my word just right. Besides, I didn't want to hurt her. I loved her! Somehow I had to protect her from the truth that I was twisted and self-absorbed.

"It was you! Because they played a recording, they had ask your name and you(me)," Said Rick. "Don't lie. Why would you do this?"

I had no answers other then we'll talk when I get home. That day was long, and that night, well, it was longer. I knew I had been busted. I had to plead ignorance and remorse.

She made claims that it was no different than if I had physically cheated. I didn't agree with that, still, how could I possibly refute what she was saying? In the end, she informed me that didn't need to happen again. She had lied saying she didn't recognize the voice—my voice on the recording. She knew we financially couldn't pay out that kind of money. She sure didn't want the kids to find out that their dad would do something like this. So she lied to cover my failure to commit to her and our marriage. I was either to blind to see or to dumb to realize, that I had caused a lot of damage to our marriage. Lisa's trust in me had been greatly damaged, and I was sorry. Question was, was I sorry for my actions or was I only sorry that I had gotten caught? Only time would tell. Somehow I had to get a grip on myself and my actions!

After that, I refrained from engaging in any of my self gratify actions. I was honestly fearful of what Lisa might do. You don't understand; I *loved* my wife. I didn't want to hurt her, and I had. I needed to fix this, but how?

It was a rocky road to get back in Lisa's good graces. I had shaken our marriage to the very core.

Due to Lisa's past, it was hard for her to trust people, which in itself compounded my betrayal. What I have come to understand while writing this, as it has been like reliving my past, except now I see with new eyes all the hurt and pain that I caused. While in my heart, I've always loved my wife and kids. I worked hard to give them a good life to provide them with things. Did I really know and understand the meaning of "Love"?

I don't believe that I genuinely valued them to be more precious than life itself. Please don't read that wrong, understand that I would have, even now, I would do anything in the world for my wife and kids. I was lost and searching for that missing element. Not even realizing that I was lost, sure I knew I was living in sin, I just didn't care. I believed that I would find peace and tranquility in some form of sexual experience.

All those years, I lived in my own world on the corner of lies and denial—a world ruled by me, myself, and I. It was a world where I did no wrong and others were allowed in, only to serve and make my life more comfortable.

It wasn't going to be easy. I just knew that despite everything I had done, I didn't want to lose my Lisa. Honestly, I'm not sure if things actually got better or if I just got really good at hiding my issues.

The Return

From the very beginning, Lisa and I, for the most part, have always done everything together. Neither one of us seemed to have the type of friends that had a guys' or girls' night out. Maybe it would have been better if we had. Then again, depending on the type of friends they were, that may have created more issues. The good Lord only knows I didn't need any more help in destroying my marriage.

Still, I can't help but wonder, even in those times that we were together, going somewhere or doing something. No matter the quality even if it was grocery shopping, it was still time spent together. Right? Had that in some way helped hold us together?

Lisa had quit her job and picked up a few houses to clean, which was a good thing. It made her schedule more flexible between the kids, their school activities, and my work schedule. One day, when we were both off work, Lisa and I went out and about. We were looking around at our local mall when we ran into an old friend. He had gone to Bible College with Lisa, and he remembered all the issues that we had with my parents. But then again, who didn't know about our dating controversy with my parents?

At some point in our conversation, he asked the dreaded question on where were we going to church. Well, we weren't going to lie, we simply told him we weren't. Like any loving and caring person, he shared about where he was attending. They had just accepted a new pastor. They were a young family close to our age and on fire for God. "You need to come and check it out," he said. As he gave us the church's address.

Lisa and I talked about it, maybe we did need to get back in church. It wasn't like we didn't know any better, after all, church was the foundation our marriage was based on. And we knew that the way we were living was wrong. Speaking for myself, I just didn't really care anymore. Christianity had just been something that I consistently failed at. In the past, I had done everything that I thought was right, reading my Bible, spending time in prayer, attending church, and serving when the opportunity presented itself. The result was always the same when I faced the temptation of sexual struggles, *I always failed*! Besides, I was to busy doing what made me feel good—although, that in itself, wasn't working out too well for me.

I believe one of the hardest things for a person to do is to make that initial step—to walk into a church for the first time—even if you know at least a few of the people there, it's still hard!

As we sat in the car, waiting for that perfect time to walk in, you know when Sunday school is over and everyone was moving into the sanctuary for church. That way, if we were lucky, we would be lost in the crowd, blending in. Like you can really get lost in a crowd of eighty people. While we did time things well for our entrance, still there were several people that knew us, and we received a warm reception.

Our friend was right, the minister was good! There seemed to be something different about him, he seemed genuine, more relatable. As the weeks went by, we began to once again regularly attend church. While it wasn't at the same time, Lisa and I both gave our lives back to God, repenting of our sinful life and rededicating our lives to Christ. A new and fresh start serving Jesus had begun.

We both jumped right in, helping any way we could. It wasn't long before Lisa began teaching a children's Sunday School class. While I did have to work every other weekend, I had days off during the week. The pastor invited me to go with him to a pastors' weekly prayer time on Wednesdays when I was off. It was an open format, just several like-minded pastors with a desire for more of God. Desiring revival, they were hungry for more, and so was I!

I grew in that time! I also enjoyed the fact that ministers of different churches could and would come together. Not one minister claimed to have it all figured out, in fact, they would help and pray for each other. Lifting other churches up in prayer. I believe that is what Christ wants us to do in His Church. There was unity unlike anything I had seen in the past, and it gave me new hope.

There were times that I was able to go with our pastor on hospital visitations. It felt like I was becoming a part of actual ministry. The more I could do, the more that ole flame would burn. I knew that God had a purpose for me, that purpose He had given me years ago—the one that I dodged to make Lisa and my life together, easier.

It was an early fall day when I tagged along with pastor as he traveled over to the Bible college. That's the same one I had grown up around, the very one Lisa had attended when we were dating. We left early enough to sit in on their morning chapel service. Afterward, Pastor, myself, and the superintendent of the school went to a little cafe just to talk. While I really don't remember a whole lot about the conversation, I do remember the superintendent brought up the fact the school was in need of another cook. *Remember* what I said about Lisa and her cooking abilities? That's when I put in that Lisa may be interested in cooking there, and I could mention it to her, which they thought would be great. I had also mentioned the fact that I would like to sit in on some classes on my days off.

I had a new excitement as I went home that day, sharing the mornings' events with Lisa, eager for her reaction. While she had questions, she was interested. It wasn't long after that when she began to make that trip in the early mornings, Monday through Friday. There, she would cook breakfast and help start preparing for lunch and supper.

I would spend my mornings that I was off in classes, depending on the class schedule. There were times that I would get off work after a twelve-hour shift and go over to catch a couple of classes.

It had it's challenges but we made it through that year. Most of those attending Bible college were kids just out of high school. There were three of us that was a little older who felt the call of ministry on our life. Now I know that we are all called to be ministers of God's word. This was more specific, to be either a pastor or evangelist.

That summer, Lisa and I help at their church youth camp. This was the same youth camp that I had attended. My pastor allowed me to preach on several occasions for the Sunday evening services. He also had connections with a small independent Christian radio station. We split the cost and filled a slot on Saturday afternoons. Alternating weeks, it was nothing like what's available now, podcasts and live streaming on Facebook. We would go into the church and prerecord our message, and then he would drop the tape off at the radio station.

There were a lot of prayers going up that summer for direction, as we continued to seek the will of God for our life. Seeking to know His will, was I to quit my job and go to college full time, and if so how do I take care of my responsibilities and provide for my family and pay our bills? Sure, the college had a house available for a family. It was questionable if they would even allow us to live there. We knew that there was at best a strained relationship with some of the faculty members. See I had questioned certain ideas that didn't quite line up with scripture. God is a big God, His word is a living word. There's more to being a Christian than by following a set of rules based on how others interpret the scriptures. That can fall into simply being religious and not having a personal relationship with Jesus.

Things were even better with my parents. We were at least talking and would go over to their house to visit regularly. They actually began to come over to our house on several occasions as well.

Lisa and I agreed that we should test the waters and put our new home up for sale. This didn't come as easy because she loved our house. Despite some of my actions and memories, it had become our home. It wasn't long and someone else fell in love with our home, and we closed the deal and sold our house.

We didn't have a place to live, so we ended up renting a house. It wasn't in the best location, but we knew it was just temporary. And it gave us the flexibility should something open up that we needed to relocate we didn't have ties with a house.

As we planned on returning for a second year at the Bible College, we knew that Lisa had already committed to cooking there for the upcoming semester and I would attend classes again. That August, before college started, they held a "camp meeting." There was one-afternoon service the three of us from last year were each given twenty minutes to deliver a message. It was a way of introducing to that church movement (denomination) of possible soon to be ministers. It went well for all three of us. I was given several opportunities to preach at different churches that were affiliated with the college. They were all within forty miles of home.

With a family, I was still working, and Lisa was cooking there while we were still living 18 miles away. We had heard that a church in our movement, in Texas, was seeking a pastor. With that, I wrote a brief resume and dropped it in the mail. It wasn't long before we were invited out to preach. It was just the way things were done. They would have different candidates come to preach, similar to an interview. The church board and members would want to meet the entire family. That way the congregation could see if they liked the candidate who was being considered in becoming their pastor and to see if the candidate and their family were interested in pastoring them. Simply put, they wanted to make sure it was a good fix for everyone involved.

It was a fairly long trip as Lisa, myself, and both our kids left early that Saturday

OUR STRUGGLES ARE REAL!

morning. We would arrive early that evening. The town was smaller than the one I had grown up in, which wasn't an issue, not if that's where God wanted us! Their head board member welcomed us into her home. She showed us around the church and parsonage. We returned to her home where she had a home-cooked meal prepared for us and gave us a place to stay that night.

As I reviewed the message that God had laid on my heart, I had a confidence and a sense of peace about delivering it. That's not to say I wasn't nervous, but I knew once I began, God would calm me as I allowed His Spirit to speak through me.

That Sunday morning, service went well. As it appeared that the message was well-received, the people were all positive. As we left that day to go home, Lisa and I both were confident in the way things had gone. We said a little prayer for our journey home and that God's will be done in our lives. If it's meant to be, God would open the door.

Preaching Gods Word

I'm not sure the reason, but one Sunday morning, we went to church with my parents. (Again, the church and college are tied in together.) As we were leaving the church, the pastor there asked if I would bring the message that night. Now I had made a little promise to God about opportunities to teach and preach. When asked, the answer is yes, unless I already have a commitment. So I gladly accepted as I began to pray for the message that God would have me bring.

I spent that afternoon in prayer and study, preparing for that evening service. While nervous, I was confident of the message for that evening, I still remember what it was that I shared so boldly.

> Wearing a linen ephod, David was dancing before the Lord with all his might, while he and all Israel were bringing up the ark of the Lord with shouts and the sound of trumpets. As the ark of the Lord was entering the City of David, Michal daughter of Saul watched from a window. And when she saw King David leaping and dancing before the Lord, she despised him in her heart. They brought the ark of the Lord and set it in its place inside the tent that David had pitched for it, and David sacrificed burnt offerings and fellowship offerings before the Lord. When David returned home to bless his household, Michal daughter of Saul came out

to meet him and said, "How the king of Israel has distinguished himself today, going around half-naked in full view of the slave girls of his servants as any vulgar fellow would!" David said to Michal, "It was before the Lord, who chose me rather than your father or anyone from his house when he appointed me ruler over the Lord's people Israel—I will celebrate before the Lord. I will become even more undignified than this, and I will be humiliated in my own eyes. But by these slave girls you spoke of, I will be held in honor." And Michal daughter of Saul had no children to the day of her death. (2 Samuel 6:14–17, 20–23, NIV)

King David had brought the Ark back into the Temple, God's house, and the passion and the zeal that he demonstrated. How he passionately rejoiced! He held nothing back! He was extremely excited and he, let it show.

His wife, the daughter of ex-king Saul, called him out on how he had rejoiced and worshiped, undignified. Because of her attitude, her belief that David was wrong, in his actions, and as a result of her actions, it was she that became barren, unable to have children. I related it to how we should be excited about Jesus and the freedom that only He can bring in our lives. It was a strong message, that I believe is still true today! I had delivered with such a passion.

I remember my favorite teacher, sitting and intently listening. His occasional "amens" were encouraging throughout the message. Afterward, he gave me some positive feedback, and again I was even more encouraged. Even today, I stand behind that message!

Like all good things, there comes opposition. Not everyone shares the same views, which is fine. *Always remember*, when it comes to a message or sermon, whether you are giving it or hearing it, make sure it lines up with scripture—even if it means reading a chapter or two both before and after your selected scripture. Just a few words or the setting can change an entire meaning.

I had shared what had God laid on my heart. I didn't compromise or water it down. If I was given the opportunity to give that message again, I wouldn't change a thing.

I just didn't realize the storm that was brewing in our life, and it was about to pour down!

It was an exciting feeling that we were stepping into God's purpose for our life. We were a little puzzled, and there was a sense that something was off around the college. Since Lisa was there every morning in the kitchen, she was more in tune with the everyday pulse of things.

A couple of weeks had passed since I had preached the sermon on David and the Ark. I was a little surprised when the superintendent asked if I had time that he would like to speak with me. I didn't have anything else going on that day, and he said he had time around lunch. As I walked in and sat down, we casually talked about how things were going.

Then he asked if I knew why I hadn't been selected as the pastor for the church in

Texas. *I'm sorry I forgot to mention the letter.* I had received a letter thanking us for coming; however, they had felt lead to go with someone else, which in reality I think was an answer to Richard and Bethany's prayers. Lisa and I were a little disappointed, but if that's God's will, okay!

"Evidently it wasn't God's will, as the time there, I felt had gone well," was the answer I gave. He then proceeded to explain that my resume was poorly written. He personally knew the lady that we had stayed with, and that she was a retired schoolteacher. How I should have had someone help me write my resume, which I understood to a point, but the fact was that resume did get me an "interview," so to speak.

It was a constant barrage of criticism and he was just softening things up before he addressed the real reason for this conversation. He proceeded to ask about my message that I had preached about King David. He expressed how I had totally missed it! As he informed me that originally, he was supposed to preach that night. It had bothered him as he had the message God wanted to be delivered that night. But the opportunity had been taken away from him. How he had thought that it might be all right, if I had truly been in tune with God then I would have had the same message he had. And the message I had brought "*was not the message* from God for that night."

It was like someone had knocked the wind right out of me. Surprisingly, I kept my composure, remaining confident that I had allowed God to lead and direct my words that night. He was like an alpha male on the attack, and he wasn't backing down, the thing was, neither was I. There had been some things talked about in class and discussed around the dining hall tables from time to time. I had expressed a certain amount of reservation on how some things were taught. My personal thoughts and convictions—I wasn't the only one—was that some of the faculty members were closed-minded. So set in their beliefs that God Himself wouldn't be able to change their minds. Now I agree unwavering faith is *awesome*! However, the Bible is the Word of God, His living word. His word never changes however our understanding should continually grow deeper.

I continued to explain that the message was what God had laid on my heart. I wasn't going to apologize for what God had laid on my heart. Just because we may view scripture differently, doesn't mean he's right and I'm wrong or I'm right and he's wrong. It's that we are all at different points in our walk with Christ. Depending on our individual walk and where we are at spiritually, depends on what depth the Holy Spirit will reveal things to us. How else can we explain a passage of scripture we have read multiple times? Then, one day, it's like being in a pitch-black room when all of a sudden someone turned on the lights. We have a much clearer understanding, and God will stretch us, but He won't overwhelm us. Isn't that the purpose of ministry, to help others grow deeper spiritually.

The superintendent was firm in his belief that I did not deliver God's message that evening! Never once did he offer any suggestion of what the message was "supposed to be." I felt personally attacked, perhaps I shouldn't have, but it seemed like one blow after another. I knew I was running a certain amount of risk by voicing my convictions. Sorry but not sorry, there are other people that can hear from God. I know I wasn't backing down. I knew in my spirit I had followed God's leading. I just wasn't willing to compromise what God had laid on my heart. I proceeded to simply ask questions. If we believe the scripture to be the inspired word of God, how come we pick and choose? Why do we believe God only works in our movement and not others?

Then things got specific. I bought up certain manifestations—some believe in being slain in the Spirit. Now I'm not saying it is or isn't of God. I did, however, use this passage of scripture:

> As he neared Damascus on his journey, suddenly a light from heaven flashed around him. He fell to the ground and heard a voice say to him, "Saul, Saul, why do you persecute me?" "Who are you, Lord?" Saul asked. "I am Jesus, whom you are persecuting," he replied. "Now get up and go into the city, and you will be told what

you must do." The men traveling with Saul stood there speechless; they heard the sound but did not see anyone. Saul got up from the ground, but when he opened his eyes he could see nothing. So they led him by the hand into Damascus. For three days he was blind, and did not eat or drink anything. (Acts 9:3–9, NIV)

Saul had been knocked off his horse, falling to the ground, and as He lay there, he encountered God.

In an angry and offended voice, the superintendent asked, "Is that what that means?"

I wasn't trying to create a bigger argument, as I simply posed a question. In my own thoughts, *I believe that's what happened to Saul*. "I'm just asking the question if that's a possibility?" Our conversation had come to an impassable level of conflict. There was only one way in his mind—that was his way. I was *wrong* in my thoughts, my message was *wrong* on that Sunday evening, and I wasn't smart enough to dazzle my words in a resume.

As I left that day, I experienced a wide range of emotions—upset, angry, and disappointed. I felt unworthy and heavily condemned. It didn't matter that I still had my secret struggles. Yes, even while studying God's word, preaching on occasion. I periodically felt sexual pressure, so I found relief. I didn't use my old means of movies and magazines. I would just masturbate while in the shower. That evening, I was fueled by my hurt and anger. Digging down in my memories, fantasizing of being wanted, even needed. I once again gave myself that carnal pleasure that I had so often fell into.

As I finished my shower that feeling of guilt, shame, and unworthiness washed over me once again. I immediately knelt down at the side of our bed and repented.

Over the next couple of weeks, I tried to continue with my classes. Things were different—even several of the teachers would talk with me differently. I guess it's only normal for teachers to talk. I'm just not sure, but because he was the superintendent shouldn't he maintain a higher standard, I don't believe that he should have been talking about our conversation. I am positive that he had painted me to be a heathen, unwilling to listen and simply go along with his views. After all, he was just trying to give guidance and shed light on my lack of knowledge.

It didn't matter what had happened with me, Lisa still had her responsibilities of cooking. I realize now how selfish my reaction was. Regardless, I gradually stopped attending classes, encouraging Lisa to just quit as well, which she eventually did. Oh, she gave them a notice, that allowed them to fill her position before she left. I know that it was wrong for me to expect her to give up something she enjoyed. I felt they didn't really want me there anyway. Plus the little comments that Lisa had heard, both directly and indirectly. Besides, in my way of thinking, if they did really care, someone would have reached out, expressing a level of concern for the matter, which is another reason why I believed the superintendent had "blackballed" me.

Our pastor was confused as well by the superintendent's actions. He wasn't so opinionated, but he was willing to keep an open mind. I think he believed that while the superintendent was probably in the wrong, I may have pushed the envelope just a little too far. I didn't expect him to intervene on my behalf—that could just make things hard on him, especially since he had a family.

I didn't understand how I had failed God and missed His plan for our life. After we had sacrificed our new home, I was confused, but I didn't just quit serving God. Right or wrong, honestly it was wrong, but we left that church since they were part of that movement affiliated with the college.

As I look back on that conversation, neither one of us acted mature. I do still feel that he had alternatives motives. I continued to seek God, but it didn't seem like there was a place for me. As I still had connections with some of the pastors from the pastor's prayer, we visited several of their churches. Nothing or no place was a true fit or would satisfy that deep inner being, the desire to share and do God's work. Unlike before, I was earnestly seeking God's will this time, but nothing. My heart seemed empty. I questioned my purpose, my life, and my calling. My world, my faith, and everything that I come to believe in had been shaken to the very core.

Twisted and Confused

Our son, Richard, was in high school now. He was actively involved with band, marching band, and choir. When somehow, he started going to a church service on Friday nights.

At that time, there was a big revival 180 miles away, and it had been going for several months at least. There was a young man that was from the church where the revival was happening. He and another guy had started doing the Friday night service, focusing on youth to young adults.

Hungry for more of God, to allow Him to touch and change lives, their desire was to bring what was happening there, here. Their pastor was in full support of this pursuit of God. Often, the church leadership would travel there to attend the revival services in hopes of bringing a part of that fire back.

As the weeks passed, Richard regularly attended those Friday night services. He always came home excited, talking about God stirring hearts and lives and how we should at least check it out. Sure that, we would encounter God!

One week, when I was off and didn't have to go to work the next day, we all went. It was *awesome*. The presence of God was there. Somehow, it seemed more tangible than I had ever experienced. It wasn't long, and we too were attending regularly, including going to the church's Sunday service. It would appear we had found our place—everyone was so friendly and inviting. And it wasn't just the leadership, it was the entire congregation that was hungry for a move of God. The Spirit of God was certainly in that place!

Lisa had picked up some house cleaning jobs to make some extra money. Bethany was about to start high school herself. Now the church had a Christian school there also. As we visited with the pastor who was also the principal, we toured the classrooms. Since Richard was already active in high school he wanted to continue in public school. Bethany was a different story showing an interest in attending the private Christian school. Lisa and I decided that would be able to financially make it work. Since Lisa's job was extra income, Bethany's tuition wouldn't be a problem.

We were once again actively serving God and we had made some lifelong friendships. There were ways that stretched us. Like I stated earlier, I try to have an open mind, not to put God and His possibilities in a box.

Bethany was excelling in her schoolwork and her walk with Christ. Some of the youth had a praise and worship team. She had sung at church before, and now she picked up a guitar and began to learn that too.

As we became more active, we ourselves went with a small group to that revival 180 miles away. You definitely knew that the Spirit of God was there. Coming into His presence as He poured out in a new and refreshing way.

All this time, I so wanted a mighty move of God in my life. Something that was so real it was unmistakably God. I didn't have him in a box. I wasn't limiting Him in any way. I have seen, even talked, with different ones that had experienced His goodness. Even my wife had those encounters, so what was wrong with me? I would receive prayer, and as people prayed over me, they spoke heartfelt words—words that targeted areas in my life that I hadn't shared. I so want the power of God to strike. It was courtesy drop after courtesy drop, and as I would lay there, I prayed and pleaded with God.

Was it possibly the walls in my life were impenetrable? Had I allowed all the hurt and disappointments to harden me? Was I holding on to anger and bitterness? During my teen years, I was compassionate and caring, and even tender moments, that I would shed a tear. Perhaps it was in part due to growing up in the sheltered environment that I was resentful for. As life progressed, I had learned life was cold, hard, and even unfair; and that people would knock you out of the way, make fun of, or just step on you to accomplish their goals.

At some point, I began to "man up" and stopped being so sensitive. Refusing to shed a tear, I didn't realize that my heart had become that hard. And I'm not sure I was ready to allow God to do what was necessary.

> I will give them an undivided heart and put a new spirit in them; I will remove from them their heart of stone and give them a heart of flesh.
> (Ezekiel 11:19 NIV)

It's one thing for people to treat you harshly, often taking advantage of a kind and caring heart. But when those people, people that call themselves "Christians" are manipulating, that's sinking to a whole new level.

It's not like I didn't know the scripture:

> In your anger do not sin:
> Do not let the sun go down while you are still angry.
> (Ephesians 4:26, NIV)

I thought that I had let go of things, that I wasn't holding on to an anger and bitterness. Or so I thought, but I knew that to go back and have another conversation with the Bible College superintendent would just end up in a confrontation. To which I would be construed as trying to force my convictions off on them. After all, "he (the superintendent) was just trying to help me." I was trying my best to walk the conflict in our lives, out in faith. And it wasn't just the Bible college thing, there was the roller coaster ride with my parents. Shortly after the Bible college incident, we had yet another blow up with my parents. As I think back, I try to remember the details of why. I can't give the specifics, I just know they always ended up wanting to be controlling of our lives. It just seemed never-ending, there was always something.

I think that I had accepted masturbation as just a part of a guy's life. It in itself wouldn't be so wrong, would it? After all, it's just a type of pressure relief valve. And I wasn't looking at adult magazines or watching adult movies for visual aide anymore. Yeah, sure there was the occasional young woman in the tight short, shorts, or the woman that was, shall we say "top-heavy" wearing a skin-tight, low cut top. I just couldn't help but notice and then notice again. You know, just to be sure you saw what you thought you saw. Besides, isn't it uplifting, a confidence booster, when you compliment someone? Either I was just twisted in my thoughts or could it possibly be normal? How confusing!

Our family was doing well. We were generally always busy between work, working out, the kids' activities, and church. If I'm honest, I had begun to slip back in my Christian walk. Instead of taking my thoughts captive, my thoughts began to once again take me captive.

Despite any confusion that I faced, it was rewarding that Lisa, Richard, and Bethany appeared to be drawing closer to God. Appearances, however, can be so deceiving!

The church and school wanted to do some type of mission trip. I know, we always think of going to a foreign country as a mission field. The sad fact is, this great country of ours has plenty of opportunities.

They had contacted a church in Louisiana and began to plan for a five-day mission trip. As they organized the trip, they wanted a balance of youth and adults. With the way my schedule was, I didn't feel that we could afford for me to take off work. Sure Lisa and I had talked about going, we knew it really would be a good experience. We did the math and figured that we could swing the financial cost. However, with Bethany attending the school, it was almost expected that she go, besides she really wanted to go anyway. So we decided that Bethany and Lisa should be the ones to go, at least from our family.

What happened next began a downward spiral in my life. Unfortunately, it becomes so easy for us to see men and women that follow God and place them on a pedestal. We forget that they're only human, and as men and women, we have a tendency to stumble. That's why we must focus on Christ, always making Him the center of our life—because if we don't, we become like Peter. When we take our eyes off Jesus, even if it's only for a moment, we begin to sink. It's in those moments that we stumble, that we must recognize that we have fallen. We face choices every day, do we chose to lay there in defeat or do we get up and press on?

It's because of God's grace and love that enables us to get back up. Too many times, I hear people use God's grace as an excuse to sin. It's not because of grace that I can sin and God will forgive. It's because of grace that when we fall short, we can call out to God, seeking Him with a repentant heart that He will extend His grace bringing about our forgiveness. His grace picks us up, brushes us off, teaches us the areas that are sin and desires that we don't continue to stumble over the same things repeatedly.

Jesus declared. "Go now and leave your life of sin." John 8:11 NIV

Grace is for when we fall, NOT so that we can purposely fall.

The superintendent of the Bible college, the two young men, and the pastor of the church trying to perusing "revival." I had set them up on a pedestal. I hadn't intended to idolize them, they just appeared to be so focused. Living Christ-centered, Godly lives, and a pattern—an example that I could set for my life.

It seems that I have fallen so many times. I had reached a point that I questioned my sincerity. Why was I constantly make the same mistakes over and over again? Although they weren't the same, they were a progression, steadily sinking deeper.

Lisa and Bethany left with the mission group on Sunday after church. As it would happen, that was my weekend that I was working days. Now when you work a twelve to thirteen-hour shifts all a person feels like doing is eat, sleep, and go to work, repeat. At least that's how I felt—I didn't have a day off till Tuesday that week.

With the girls gone and Richard driving, I could actually sleep in. I got up on Tuesday, done a few things around the house, and went to the gym to get my workout in. Something felt off that day as I went through my work out. The weight of frustration, perhaps I did miss not having Lisa around. Even if we didn't work out side by side, it was just the knowing that she was near.

There wasn't anyone there at the gym that morning, at least that I knew. True, it was late morning, and I usually was there much earlier. That's when I noticed a woman working out on the weight machines. Now I usually always used the free weights, on occasion I would use the machines. Point is from the area I was at you could see the machine weights area.

She was attractive, and her tight workout attire was complimentary of her figure. We noticed each other several times, which made it obvious that we were checking each other out. As I went to work out on a nearby machine, I casually spoke to her. I could tell there was a certain amount of mutual physical attraction. I just wasn't sure of how or even if I wanted to pursue her.

I began having thoughts of Lisa, how I really did love her, but then thoughts of this gal. I dismissed my fleshly desires as I thought that she was probably out of my league. I had always talked a good game, but this was an actual person. As I finished my work out, I got up the nerve to approach her to engage in a conversation. As I scanned the room, I couldn't find her. She had evidently finished her workout and left.

It was confusing to me how I had wanted to make sexual advances yet I was so fearful. Was it because I knew it was wrong, that it would be wrong for me to do, as I'm married and I do love my wife? Or was it that I was just afraid of being rejected, exposed or making a fool of myself? It didn't matter, she was gone, and I could go home to an empty house.

There, I would fantasize about how that afternoon may have gone if I had only been a confident "player." I replayed that morning over, again and again, rehearsing in my mind how I would act and what I would say and do—if ever given the chance. Yes, those thoughts had aroused my sense of pleasure and the pursuit of adventure. Once again, I achieved the release of that sexual tension as I took a hot shower.

Now you would think that by pleasuring myself, I would be relieved of my sexual desires. That those tensions would cease at least for a few days. However, as I awoke the next morning, the thought that maybe the mystery woman would be at the gym today, perhaps about the same time as yesterday. I geared my morning to be around and at the gym at the same time as yesterday. I had even talked with Lisa and had told her that I was going to go workout that morning.

I was nervous, maybe even scared as I tried to do my workout that day. I couldn't focus. I just watched the area I had seen her the day before. I was about to give up when she showed up. Then new fears set in, but my adrenaline kick in. After our eye locked a couple of times, I struck up a conversation. Introducing myself, I ask her if she would like to get lunch after our workout. To my surprise, she accepted.

We meet up in the lobby area after we showered and changed. We agreed where we should go, and she followed me to a nearby sandwich shop where we talked about our lives. She was recently divorced and had two kids, her ex-husband had been a real jerk. As she asked me my story, I told her what I thought she wanted to her, I told her things about my life as close to the truth as I could. My wife and I had been struggling in our marriage and was currently separated—*not* at all a *lie*! Colored with the need for someone that understands, it must have worked because as we finished our lunch, she invited me to follow her back to her place.

It seemed like it took forever to get there as my heart raced. I had determined that I was going to go through with satisfying my lustful needs and desires. Once there, she drew the blinds closed as we sat on her living room couch. We soon found ourselves entangled in each other's arms. Then it quickly advanced to us both being topless, lying on the living room floor. She asked if I had protection. What, wait? Sure I knew what she meant, but I didn't. I hadn't even thought this through completely. Now to go get "protection" would totally ruin the moment. But without it, that was a deal-breaker for her. She was going to have her kids that evening, but we could get together around mid-morning the next day.

As I left, I was more flustered than ever. So close, sure most guys would have forced the issue. That's never been me, but then again, most guys would have been more prepared.

Now it was Thursday and I had to work the night shift. I would normally lie down around 11:00 a.m. and get up after about a four-hour nap. That was going to have to wait as I returned to her house that morning. This time, I came prepared!

This time, however, we didn't even go in the house. As we sat on the back porch, she explained that she didn't want to be "that woman." Since my wife and I was only separated and not divorced, that's what sealed her and her ex-husband's fate was another woman.

Nothing I could say or do was going to change her mind. Once again, I left frustrated, feeling inadequate as a man and unable to "close the deal," *Failure*. How was it possible to have so many conflicting emotions spinning through my mind? Did women not find me attractive enough, or was I not confident enough? Loneliness, emptiness, worthless as a "man," angry, alone, guilt, and worthless as a husband, full of shame, and feeling ashamed, and defeated. With all these emotions, I still hungered for raw and lust-filled sex. I wasn't wanting a relationship with ties. There was this seemingly unsatisfiable desire for the ultimate sexual encounter. My biggest question was what was wrong with me? Why could I not make that connection?

Once again I found myself home alone taking a hot shower. No, she wasn't there in the physical body, but mentally I found my sexual release I had desired with her.

A New Low

Sure all those sexual urges remained a constant in my life, but I wasn't about to force myself on anyone. I knew what I was doing was wrong on multiple levels. I did have a level of fear that I would get caught. I knew that I didn't want to lose Lisa or my family, I really did love them. Still, there was a burning desire, that raged deep within me. It was that same week that I had to make a trip to the store.

As I walked across the parking lot, a nearby payphone rang. My heart raced as I answered it, "Hello."

She proceeded to ask sexual suggestive questions and make comments. I tried to get her number, suggesting that maybe we could meet, maybe she would be interested in doing more than just talk. There was silence as the line went dead, and she had rung up.

I'd played her game in an attempt to take it to the next level. The phone rang again, the talk continued, only briefly before once again, she was gone. Now, more frustration set in along with fear coupled with a certain amount of excitement. Not knowing exactly who was on the other end of that phone call, was she who she said she was, was she of legal age? It could have even been the police.

I had no intentions before my wife and daughter had gone on the mission trip of having any kind of sexual escapade. None whatsoever! But now all that had somehow changed. It was as if I had to make some type of conquest to redeem myself as a "man." before Lisa got home.

It was the night before they were going to be home from their mission trip. My last opportunity, probably the last time I would ever have a chance to experience sex with someone else. I can't explain it, I felt this enormous amount of pressure building up inside of me.

Richard and I had both went to bed. Lisa had already called as we had talked every evening that she was gone that week. I honestly couldn't sleep anyway, so it was a role reversal.

A NEW LOW

Instead of the kid sneaking out, I slipped out of the house. I found a secluded payphone that you didn't even have to get out of your car to use.

After I had tried to call a couple of payphone numbers that I had written down, there was no one that answered. I proceeded to call a phone sex line. I had acquired someone's credit card account information with no idea whose it was. All I knew was the account number was legit and couldn't be traced to me this time.

Entering the required numbers, I made my selection. Like I said, I could talk a good game. It wasn't about just achieving my climax and relieving my sexual pressure. It was about creating the ultimate sexual encounter. Statistics show that most of these calls are around four minutes. I'm sure the call I made that night went thirty to forty minutes. It was about trying to create that ultimate experience. As I did the deed and got myself off I hung up the phone, I knew I needed to get home.

The unexpected occurred was when I walked through the door. Evidently, Lisa had called back to let me know approximately when they would be arriving home. There, Richard was sitting in our living room, wanting to know where I've been and to let me know Lisa had been trying to get ahold of me. I had *no* options other than to lie—that had become so easy for me to do. I couldn't sleep (truth), I went for a drive (truth)—that was my story, and I was sticking to it. All truths, remember, it's all about the play on words.

As I called Lisa, she got the same story. Knowing my past, she wasn't buying it. There was going to be a discussion when she got home. I had been down this road, or should I say that I have lived on that road. I tried to make my story as close to the truth, leaving off any incriminating details, and then hold to that story. There was a conversation, and I stuck to my story. Over time, with Lisa's persistent questioning, I share about going to the store and the phone call I answered, leaving the assumption that's what had happened that night.

I know this probably sounds like a lie through everything I've done. Every selfish act attempting to satisfy my twisted desires to fill what seemed like a bottomless hole on my heart. This was fueled by a burning lust of sexual desires and the curiosity of having multiple partners. I have *always* loved Lisa!!! The intent of hurting her was absolutely the last thing I *ever* wanted to do.

To be totally transparent, I've questioned if I even knew what love was. For me to continue down the same path, continually hurting the one person that remained by my side, I had a feeling in my heart for Lisa like none other. Still, the burning desires of my flesh overran my heart. I believe it's the same type of struggle that Paul writes about in Romans 7:19 (NIV):

> For I do not do the good I want to do, but the evil I do not want to do—this I keep on doing.

Do any of us understand love and the depths that it can run? I think that's what it is, there are multiple levels of love. I remember the saying, "puppy love"—when our heart first flutters because of the way someone makes us feel. Then when we consider how deeply Christ must have loved us—to leave heaven, to walk on this earth, and to suffer and die the death He endured. Yes, undoubtedly, there are levels of love. When it came to Lisa, I knew in my heart that I loved her!

Are the things that we learned, early in life, what shapes our love? Perhaps, it simply gives us our baseline. Then as we go through life, our experiences contribute greatly to our understanding. It's only when we allow Christ to have control of our heart that's when when love begins to grow the deepest and purest forms.

Please, I'm not trying to make any more excuses for my behavior. I've done enough of that to last a lifetime twice over! While I believe my parents did love me in their idea of love, as long as I did everything I was told, things were fine. They spoiled me with privileges and material things. There was never any real communication.

Just think about your perception of God as your father. Have you ever compared God our heavenly father to our earthly father? I mean, I have! I saw my dad working hard, never really having a true relationship with me. I don't remember him ever just sitting down, sharing his heart with me, ever. He ruled our home with fear, not just with him but Mom as well—each had their different tactics. Most of the time the correction was harsh, the kind that leaves marks and bruises. So that's the perception of a father that I had to break. Relating my father with God as my father. If God is indeed love…

> Whoever does not love does not know God, because God is love. (1 John 4:8, NIV)

Then isn't it possible to develop a false value of love itself? Then there's the flip side because of what we see. It can act as a driving force that keeps you from repeating those actions that you grew up in.

After all, everything begins with a choice, that's part of free will and God's grace.

Still somehow in my mind, I honestly thought I was protecting Lisa by keeping my devious and perverse ways from her. I was telling her lies and half-truths, and they seemed easier than being open and honest. At times, it felt as if I was literally being ripped in to. Sure, there were those times that there was no denying my perversion. Yes, I was sorry, but only because I had gotten caught.

OUR STRUGGLES ARE REAL!

For years, Lisa would say that even doing the phone sex and chat lines I was cheating—that even in conversation, you are giving a part of yourself to whoever is on the other end. That you also might as well be committing the very act itself. I disagreed with that for all those years, maybe I just chose to live in denial. Then there was another side of me that heard that since I've talked the talk, I may as well physically do the deed. After all, to Lisa, there really wasn't any difference.

That's what I mean, a play on words. Justifying anything, making my actions "because of" someone else' and never being responsible for me or my actions.

Lisa's been through so much in her life. She didn't deserve the abuse that I put her through. Don't call it anything else but what it was, it was a form of abuse. When we meet, it was the compassionate me she fell in love with. Not the monster that was consumed by an unsatisfiable and selfish lust. She has always been the faithful one! There are no words that can describe how sorry I am for my actions. In the confines of this book, the worst of my story is yet to come.

A NEW LOW

Lisa was constantly questioning me about where I had been and just what I did on that night. Finally, I confessed, just not in its entirety, my story. As I couldn't sleep, I went for a drive and ended up at the store. I explained how I had answered the payphone and had a limited conversation and how there had been no physical sexual activities.

That alone was enough to break her heart. Her words went something like, "That's just wrong on so many levels and I needed help." As she cried, her tears crushed me. I did not want to lose her. I knew she had every right to kick me out and file for a divorce. I made promises in an attempt to get back into her good graces.

It was shortly after that when I began to meet with an older gentleman as an accountability partner. He and his family attended church with us. In fact, their son was in the same grade level as our daughter. He was more a father figure to several of the guys, myself included. We both opened up and shared, even though I held back on the depth that I had sunk. It seemed to help some, and at least I had a friend. Someone that was willing to sit down and listen as a mentor/disciple. He was sharing many of his own personal experiences.

For me, perhaps, I came to understand for the first time, I hadn't faced *anything* new to mankind. But my walls were strong, high, and reinforced. By the definition, I was an addict, I just hadn't realized it yet. I still didn't grasp onto how great God's love is for me. I didn't relate to God as a good father. Instead, he was a father that ruled over and corrected us. After all, that's was how my earthly father was. So, that's how I related to the who, what and how my heavenly father was.

Thing was, between my schedule and his, it was difficult to meet on a regular basis. I believe we met for a total of three maybe four times. I figured that was good enough especially since it was hard for us to get together. It was me that didn't push to continue meeting. I could have at least called him any time I needed it if I wanted, but I didn't. I think we met just long enough to appease Lisa, but I honestly did think that I'd be okay.

Casting Stones

The old saying, "Boys will be boys," will possibly always ring true. It was during his senior year of high school when Richard hit his rebellious age. He had remained friends with several of the boys at the Christian school. They would hang out and go places together, but he also had several girlfriends during that year. Unlike my parents, as long as he was in church and maintained his grades, he was okay. That's not to say if he got out of line, and we found out there weren't consequences because there was.

The issue was the pastor/principal and the two Friday night leaders. The Friday night leaders had spent time with Richard, did they not know his heart and his struggles? He had been to their house several times, and besides, they weren't that much older themselves. Had they not talked enough to really know his heart and his struggles? Perhaps they had done all the talking themselves and had failed to genuinely listen to him. Had they forgotten the struggles that a teenage boy has?

Their biggest issue; with Richard, along with anyone else, was they expected everyone to conform to those in leadership's, convictions. Yes, God has laid out what sin is; however, not everything is in black and white! It was dajavo all over again. Look at what Paul says as he wrote to the Philippian church.

> Therefore, my dear friends, as you have always obeyed—not only in my presence, but now much more in my absence—continue to work out your salvation with fear and trembling, for it is God who works in you to will and to act in order to fulfill his good purpose. (Phil. 2:12–13, NIV)

Too often, we fail in the "working out our own salvation" by following what the scripture says. Not everything in life is in black, red, and white—if it was, maybe there would be fewer issues! We must search for God's direction in our life. Spending time in prayer and reading His Word for ourselves, not relying on others to do it for us.

Probably every one of us watches television. No, I'm not saying that television's wrong, hear me out. There are a few good shows and there are some that as a Christian, I believe we have *no* business watching. I also believe that there may be some shows and movies that I feel I shouldn't watch; however, you can. That's where the working out our own salvation comes into play. Some things are based on what God has spoken to us individually, that's our convictions. Problem is, too many tend to leave off the "fear and trembling" part!

We can't take the nudging of His Holy Spirit for granted. When you feel you shouldn't do something, maybe you just shouldn't do it. Just as I also believe that we should respect other's conviction, at least when we are around them. Sometimes that may only come from being sensitive to God's Spirit. Listen for hints like a person saying,

"I'm not comfortable in whatever it may be in regards to a situation."

> Be careful, however, that the exercise of your rights does not become a stumbling block to the weak. (1 Corinthians 8:9, NIV)

To believe that one person was going to hold back a move of God, keeping Him from pouring out his Spirit? In God's timing, nothing can be stopped! If it's not meant to be, nothing can force it to happen!

In my view, they had lost their focus. I believe that's true with so many people, even churches—starting out focused, serving and seeking God, hungry for God to move and change lives. They were gradually building a barrier, almost like composing a checklist of things we must do for Him to move in "our" plans.

Don't misunderstand me, I believe their desires started off good but was their drive for more of God or to have a revival? There can be a big difference between the two. I don't believe we can pray for a copy of what's happening somewhere else. That goes with praying for a ministry like someone else's. God gives us a heart for where we are, and that comes from what we have gone through and prepares us for what we will face.

Can we learn from other's successes and failures? Most definitely, we need to be open and share our life experiences. That's just part of discipleship. It's also why I'm writing this book.

Problem was, I didn't understand this twenty years ago. I don't even think the pastor and his leadership fully grasp the concept. They had tunnel vision, so focused on God and having a "revival" in "their church" that they had forgotten about the common man and woman, the day-to-day struggles people have. You know, the ones getting up every day, going to work, punching a time clock, and where they work in the real world around real people. Life is messy. It's not like being in church or going to Bible college, where spiritually, you feel protected and built up day in and day out.

The press continued for revival while other things began to crumble. The pastor/principal had a hard line for discipline. As strict as a father that I was, even I thought that he carried things to the extreme. There were issues in the school, issues in the children's church, and issues in families' homes. I mean, who was I to cast stones, I still had my struggles. As there were all these issues, the question became how do we deal with them.

Leadership believed that as they were pressing into God, and that all these issues were just an attack from Satan to stop what God was about to do. I must agree, they were spiritual attacks! Thing is, battles can be won or lost in how we counter react, especially when we overreact.

I can't, and I won't go into detail about some of the other families issues. But when our son was called a cancer and needed to be cut out, which was impacting on both him and us. Who were these people that would forget about reaching out with love, compassion, and understanding?

It was shortly after Bethany's graduation that we left the church. This time, I was done—done with church, done with Christians (those hypocrites), and done with God (if there is one)!

The Downward Spiral

I'm sharing about the journey of my life, my struggles, and my failures. I'm being transparent about my life in hopes that whoever reads this will realize that there is hope. That they're not alone, nor do they have to go it alone. The fact is, we need help, it's even scriptural that we do help each other. I've come to stand on scriptures like:

> Therefore confess your sins to each other and pray for each other so that you may be healed. The prayer of a righteous person is powerful and effective. (James 5:16, NIV)

We should be open enough to share, confessing our struggles. Understand this, you don't need to go into ever little sorted and morbid detail. We should even confess our struggles. We should always reach out and lift others up to Jesus in prayer. We should be receiving His promises and, healing. We should understand that healing may be physical, spiritual, emotional, and/or mental.

Earlier, I stated that there have been three occasions in my life, that are difficult to share about. While I know I've been forgiven, I'll never forget. As much as I'd like to go back and change some events and things that I've done, I can't. There will always be a part of my heart that aches because of the levels that I stooped and the fact that I could hurt Lisa in the ways that I have. She would never even entertain the thought of betrayal and she has had multiple opportunities.

This is the second such occasion. It's taken me five days to just to get my mind and my thoughts together enough to begin to share. I had always planned on this event going to the grave with me.

When things started to go bad, with all the commits about Richard being a cancer, it fanned the flames of anger. After all, how do you lash out at someone that is or is at least suppose to be a man of God?" Everything was slipping! It felt as if my life was repeating. This time, it wasn't just my sexual struggles. Now in my failure to live a victorious Christian life, I had failed to be the example that my son needed me to be. I realize now I wasted so much time selfishly. There's a part of me that thinks that's even worse. In some ways, I'm guilty of dragging him down with me because of my negligence. If I had only opened up and talked with him. So many times, I had talked "at" him.

Still, there's not a one of us that wants to see our children hurt. I saw my son hurting in much the same way I had been hurt. Maybe the wording was different, but the meaning was still the same, "You're not good enough!" by hypocritical Christians in places of authority within a church.

I was still wrapped up in my world, attempting to make me feel better. Since I had discovered that you could call a payphones, it gave me an idea. Over the next month, I acquired several payphone numbers, calling them on occasion to see if and who might answer. Would they be willing to engage in a sexual conversation? Most of the time, I would find a reason or make an excuse to leave the house. I'd find a payphone that I didn't even have to get out of the car to use. Other times, just depending on my mood and time, I would stop to call a couple of the numbers on my way home from work.

Seldom did anyone ever answer, and then when someone would, it was usually a guy. What was shocking to me was the fact that even though I was a guy, more often than not, they would drop their insinuations, a guy propositioning another guy. While I could be considered a predator, with my unsatisfiable urges and tendencies, that was one boundary I wasn't willing to cross.

Then one day, she answered the payphone. As she was willing to play along, I ask if she was of legal age. This seemed to intrigue her all the more, "Just what did you have in mind?" she asked.

Problem was, she was here from a nearby town, doing some shopping with her mother and sister. If I wanted to continue this conversation, maybe even something more, I should give her a call sometime. To which she gave me her phone number, which I seriously doubted was even a legitimate number.

It was a few days later when I had that restless feeling. My heart raced as I dialed her number, and the phone rang. As a female voice answered the phone, it was her. Engaging in small talk and leading to sexual suggestions was actually as exciting for her as it was me. It was her idea that we should meet at a public spot just to see what each other looked like. Then, depending, well, we'll see.

I had told Lisa "everything" that I wanted her to know that I was going to do that day. I was both nervous and a little scared as I drove to our meeting spot. Upon my arrival, there was no one that appeared to be looking for someone that they didn't know. I hung around for a while, driving down and around the unfamiliar town. I'm not sure what I thought, neither one of us knew what type of a vehicle the other drove. As I attempted to call her, but there was no answer. Part of me was relieved, but still, I wondered what it would have been like to be with another woman.

As I was about to leave town, I decided to stop by the spot we were supposed to meet at one more time. There she was, "Are you the one I was suppose to meet earlier?" Evidently, she liked what she saw as she invited me to follow her back to her place. She was an attractive woman, in all honesty, other than her face and, dark hair, her build was quite similar to my own wife's.

At her place, we settled on the couch for small talk, which quickly lead to her bedroom. It was obvious that we both wanted the same thing. It no longer mattered that I was married, nervous, or scared. I was a man with desires, and she told me *all* the things I wanted to hear. She stroked my ego, making me feel good about myself. For the first time ever, I had actual sexual intercourse with a woman other than my wife.

As I left, we had decided that we would get together again, soon. But I had to get home as Lisa was going to be getting off work soon. I for sure didn't need to be absent when she got home. I had all day to myself, and if I wasn't there upon her arrival, she would have questions.

My mind raced full of guilt, remorse, and pleasure. I finally had the adventure that I had desired for so very long, sex with another woman. It wasn't anything special—no fireworks or total ecstasy. It was just the conquest of having *sex* with someone else who tickled my sexual fantasies with flattery.

This time I quickly forgot the guilt as I remembered Lisa's word when my phone sex activity was discovered. How that I may as well had physical sex with the person that I had talked to. It was all the same!

Notice how it was me and my choices that day, which chose to cross a line. It was a choice that destroyed the one thing that only Lisa and I had shared. How easily I justified my actions by her words. It was almost as if it was her fault.

That night, I again had a sense of conquest as I had sex with my wife. It boosted my ego even more that I had sexually performed with two women on the same day. Sure, I had thoughts, what if I had got some disease? I didn't want Lisa to suffer because of my promiscuity. She sure didn't deserve that. It just didn't matter, I was deserving and I felt empowered!

Despite all the guilt that I had, I wanted to meet up with that gal again. We talked a couple of times, even setting a date for another romp. It had felt different from the times of phone sex, this time, it did somehow feel like

I had given away a piece of me. But we have never seen each other again. It had just been a one-time thing. I used her, and she used me. Somehow, I was okay with that!

My life continued, and this time, no one was the wiser. I told myself it would never happen again, and this event would go to my grave with me.

With all the different struggles that were happening within the church, no one noticed any change in my attitude. There was almost a division between the leadership and the people. We simply went through the motions of going to church. Once Bethany graduated, we, along with several other families, faded away.

Lisa and I were in our forties. I had been in and out of church my entire life. It felt as if I had struggled with all these sexual urges equally as long. Where had it gotten me? I experienced failure after failure time and again. Certainly, I must be cursed, destined for hell. I had tried earnestly to serve God. I prayed countless hours for the deliverance from my sexual struggles. And for what? Repent, serve God, read my Bible, pray, enter temptation, pray some more, *fail*, and *repeat*.

THE DOWNWARD SPIRAL

A failure, worthless, condemned, unfaithful, a pervert—these are all words that describe how I felt about myself. I had come to believe that evidently, there was no God! If all I can do is fail, I should enjoy whatever feels good. And just like that, I was *done* going to church, and so I dragged Lisa down with me. For whatever unknown reason she was still being the "obedient" wife. I really believe she was more afraid of what I might do if she wasn't there. If there's a will, there's a way, but if she hadn't been there, I probably wouldn't be writing this now. As mad and angry as she has made me at times, it's been her love, her being by my side, not compromising her values or her moral standards that in some small way restrained me enough to keep me from going completely wild. Still, it was going to be a get in, sit down, shut up, and hold on kind of ride over the next thirteen years.

It had been about a year after we had stopped attending church, and seven years since we had come so close to losing Bethany. I had got off work that morning and stopped by the house to see Lisa before she went to work. I then headed off to the gym to get a quick workout in. I needed to get back home to go to bed as I had to work again that night. My struggles didn't seem as bad anymore. Then again maybe, I was just feeding my flesh with what I looked at or viewed. It really didn't matter that much anymore. I wasn't above just imagine my wildest fantasy and get myself off while taking a hot shower when the pressure got too much.

I was in the free weight area when someone from the front desk told me that I had a phone call. It was Lisa's boss, she had been involved in a car accident on her way to work. As I arrived at the scene, I remember thinking, *Why is her car heading the opposite direction that she should have been going?*

Now Lisa never liked that car, her description of it—it was like a "tank." That morning, she was ever so thankful for that "tank." As she had been stopped, waiting to turn, she was rear-ended by a car, traveling approximately 60 mph. The impact had spun her car around 180 degrees. While she did walk away, the impact on her body was tremendous. If you are viewing things spiritually, which at that time we weren't, God had His protecting hand over her. Also if you consider that only a month earlier we had looked at buying her a small convertible because it would have been a fun little car for her to drive, in the wreck she had, undoubtedly it would have been her death.

That next year was spent dealing with her pain and the insurance company, which was a whole different pain. It's crazy how that kind of impact can age our physical bodies, which is never taken into account with insurances. Lisa, to date, still deals with a certain amount of pain, resulting from that wreck.

After everything was settled, we decided to treat ourselves. After having both our children cesarean, Lisa decided to have an abdominoplasty done, which actually benefited me as well. I, on the other hand, made a down payment as I purchased a new motorcycle. Since both our kids were out of our house, it was time for Mom and Dad to live life and have some fun.

We soon discovered that it's not as much fun riding solo, just Lisa and I. We quickly developed new friendships with four other couples that rode too.

It seemed that we lived for the weekends that I would be off. We would go out drinking and dancing, having a good time partying. Lisa loved to dance, and she was good at it. Me, on the other hand, not so good, but I tried. Once again, there was always something pleasing for my eyes to view that would fan my sexual desires.

We made friends easily as we are both outgoing. I'm sure I know the thoughts racing through your mind and the answer is no. To be totally transparent and show to what levels I was willing to sink, sure I had thoughts of bringing another couple or even another woman into our sexual relationship. I had even brought it up on more than one occasion. My reasoning was only to strengthen our marriage, and besides, we could spice things up with some new adventures. After all, I had managed to get Lisa to watch adult movies. As things had progressed I thought that should just be the next level.

Like I said. Lisa has always maintained a certain level of integrity, never wavering from her moral compass. It didn't matter if we were in church or not her values remained consistent!

Whether they were new friends we made along the way or our small group of close friends, we were just good friends, out to have a good time; and each other's spouses were off-limits. Sure we had our joking around, insinuating a "good time," but there was never any physical sexual interaction. I will say that I used the alcohol as an excuse for a misplaced hand on more than one occasion, just not within our group.

We took bike trips together, vacationed together, and we did life together. We had developed a strong relationship with one particular couple, she and Lisa were more like sisters. It was great, and life was good. True friends who were there for us when my dad passed, and again when Lisa's brother died from brain cancer. As I wasn't able to get off work, and she flew home with Lisa to be a support—most so-called Christians won't even do that.

Tarnished

When my Dad passed, we went back over to my parents' house. I wanted to at least attempt to somehow make things right with my mom. There was a tremendous amount of work to be done around the house and business. I tried to do it all myself. My dad's half brother had been coming around quite a bit. Now I remember as a kid, hearing my parents talk about how the only time that he came around was when he wanted something, usually money. I'll just put it this way, nothing had changed. Only now they had Mom on so many different medications, it wasn't even healthy. Strange though, she was really nice. We knew it was a tough time for her, Lisa and I want to be there for her. Unlike years past, she was actually pleasant to be around. Still, we were concerned that the half brother was trying to take advantage of her, so I attempted to step in. This involved taking her to the doctor to get her medications lined out. There were multiple prescriptions from three different doctors. Needless to say, there were some medications that were actually working against each other.

You're probably thinking how something really bad could have happened. Or how it was a good thing that we cared enough to become involved in my mom's life again. While both statements are right. It's said to say, but later we came to realize it was a mistake or at least it felt that way.

As the medication began to detox from her body, the ole mom soon appeared. Her old hateful, untrusting, and angry self returned. It wasn't me that had been cheating and stealing from her, it had been dad's half brother. Sure, she had given me a little money from time to time for helping, it was never much, and I sure didn't ask her for it, nor did I expect it. That didn't matter, it was me that got the blame. I was the one that was called a thief.

Then one day, when Mom had come over to our house in the afternoon. She stayed to have supper with us as she had done several times before. We had been really trying to make things work out, and it seemed they were. It got late in the evening, so I drove Mom home in her van, eighteen miles away. Lisa followed me in her car so that I could get back home. As we neared her town, Mom began to rake Lisa over the coals verbally. What was the last straw for me was when my mom accused Lisa of cussing her out.

Now at that time in my life, I had cussed a few people out. Even now, I'm not really sure Lisa has ever really cussed anyone out. If she has, I'm fairly sure it would have been me on the receiving end. That was it, I was done, all we had done to try to help her. All the days Lisa had spent helping her in any way that she could, for mom to go back down the same road as she had years earlier, I didn't need it! Furthermore, I wasn't going to be a part of that again. I just wasn't. Nothing had changed. Despite everything I had done, I loved Lisa! I wasn't going to allow anyone to bad-mouth or hurt her in any way. It was clear that my mom's hatred for Lisa was still there.

Our party lifestyle had slowed down during the time we were trying to help mom. We had no problems picking up where we had left off. Now there was a casino nearby, drinking, dancing, and gambling all under one roof. By the clothing that most women wore, you could certainly feed your flesh. Between all the bars, casinos, and the bike rallies that we attended. Really just about anywhere we went, you can see flesh, which only continued to feed my addiction.

This is a good spot for us to talk about addictions. What I'm about to share is from what I have learned in my personal struggles. There's a lot of good information out there and some staggering statistics. As I have read several articles, I began to understand more about the demons in my life.

It seems like people automatically pair up drugs and alcohol as addictions. Because it has been a taboo subject in the church over the years, very few will address pornography and sexual issues—let alone consider them an addicting force. After all, sex is a natural part of life.

Breaking news alert—God created a man and a woman and told them to multiply. How else can we multiply unless we have sex?

> So God created mankind in
> his own image, in the image

> of God he created them; male and female he created them. God blessed them and said to them, "Be fruitful and increase in number; fill the earth and subdue it. Rule over the fish in the sea and the birds in the sky and over every living creature that moves on the ground." (Genesis 1:2–28, NIV)

Sex in its purest form was ordained by God. His primary design for marriage and sexual relations is between one man and one woman or monogamy. This is the design we see originally in the Garden of Eden. Sadly it didn't take mankind long before even sex was tarnished, filled with selfish desires and wrong motives.

In Genesis 18:20, we find the story of Sodom and Gomorrah were homosexual acts are insinuated. Then in Genesis 19:30–38, we find Lot's daughters getting their father drunk, and over two consecutive nights had sex with him without his knowledge.

All the twists and perversions of sex have been created by man in an attempt to find a greater personal pleasure, doing anything that might intensify their arousal. It was to make their desires a god as they worship both the human body and the sexual acts to satisfy themselves. It was to justify their actions under the blanket of meeting each other's needs. Love and respect for our spouse has turned into lust and expectations from anyone willing. Men and women willing to offer themselves up to fulfill either their own or someone else's desires and pleasures by any means possible. They are doing whatever it takes to satisfy themselves with no regard for biblical standards.

I've often wondered why in apostle Paul's writings, he lists so many various sexual types of sin—sexual immorality, impurity, lust, perversion, impurity, debauchery, evil desires, and greed—these are idolatry.

> Flee from sexual immorality. All other sins a person commits are outside the body, but whoever sins sexually,

sins against their own body.
(1 Corinthians 6:18, NIV)

Also, see:

- Galatians 5:19–211
- Thessalonians 4:3–51
- Corinthians10:8
- Colossians 3:5–8
- Ephesians 4:19
- Jude 1:7

Evidently, because it is one of life's pleasures, it's also one thing that God designed, you might say wired us for. Satan and his cunning and deceiving ways found a way to short circuit the human mind our desires and how we think.

The fact is, studies have proven by doing an MRI brain scan, whether its drugs, alcohol, or pornography, the images taken of the brain all look very similar. It's the release of a chemical called dopamine in our brain that gives us a rush. Dopamine is a neurotransmitter that helps control the brain's reward and pleasure centers. It is also the main part of reward-motivational behavior. The way our brain fires when we just view sexual images, how the electrons fuse together, staying bonded for up to seven days before they begin to release. As you view more images, those bond again and form an even stronger grip.

Even though our bodies can only acquire a certain level of "high," we still are constantly striving to have a more, over the top experience, and it doesn't matter what your preferred method (drugs, alcohol or sex) of pleasure is. Despite the fact, no matter what we attempt, we can only achieve a certain maximum peak experience. Feelings, such as wanting just a little more, cause us to push the limits. This causes a person using drugs to overdose. The alcoholic pushes their limits and dies from alcohol poisoning. While pornography and sexual issues doesn't physically kill it does destroy marriages, self-worth, integrity, our values. and morals.

A person can become so consumed that they no longer feel convicted as we see in

> Such teachings come through hypocritical liars, whose consciences have been seared as

with a hot iron. (1 Timothy 4:2, NIV)

Think of addiction this way—have you ever had a splitting headache? Maybe the last time you took three aspirin before you gained the desired results. The next time you have the same pounding headache, you take three of the same kind of aspirin as before. Only this time, relief doesn't come, our body has become tolerant of the dosage of three aspirin. What do we do? Take three more? We could, but at some point, what was meant for good becomes bad for us.

As I've shared, when I grew up in church, it was a *bunch* of don'ts. One of those was beer/alcohol, and while I'm not going to fault a person for drinking a beer or a glass of wine every now and then. My personal conviction for myself has evolved to abstinence from all alcohol. I heard it said that one leads to two, and two leads to too many. I was always pursuing that ultimate experience coupled with the desire of just one more time. Just one ultimate experience, and then I'll quit.

There are thousands of things we can be addicted to. Surprise! It's *not* just sex, drugs.

and rock and roll washed down with a "cold one." We can also be addicted to money, cars, homes, sports, games, and working out—to name a few. Notice how things even start as being good for us, sometimes even necessary, always full of good intentions.

You get a job, and then you begin to put more hours in taking on more responsibility in hopes of a promotion. With promotion comes more responsibility and longer hours, our dreams of providing for our family is overcome by the promise of personal power and prestige. Now we find ourselves working on the weekends to meet deadlines, thinking this could be the one. The one project that makes everyone realize just how good, how successful, how smart you are.

While chasing the dreams of making more money, having power, or being someone of importance, our children grow up. We justify missing school programs and events our children are in because we're providing them with a better life than we had. We are making empty promises that you will be there the next time. Is that suppose to makes it all better? Odds are, you just lied to your child. Is this really achieving your dreams? You know there will be something that you feel you must do or complete the next time.

Maybe you get a gym membership, planning of going forty-five minutes three times a week. As you begin to feel better and see progress, you decide to increase your time in the gym to five days a week. Now you're there for an hour. That workout burn feels good—what's another fifteen minutes? People compliment you, you catch people's attention, and you're even more confident and driven.

It's a constant push to be in good physical shape, time spent working out, eating healthy foods. We even use scripture to justify our actions.

> Do you not know that your bodies are temples of the Holy Spirit, who is in you, whom you have received from God? You are not your own. (1 Cor. 6:19, NIV)

Our addictions are our idols, as our idols have now become our addictions. We fail to realize how entangled we have become in our addiction with little desire to break away. All too often, we will mask one addiction with another.

I didn't understand that for the longest time. We make the claim that we're just more focused now. Only to enable something else to rise to the forefront of our lives—scouting, bodybuilding/working out, remodeling our home, motorcycling, and playing video games are all things that at one point consumed my/our life.

None of these things can be considered bad, and it's not a sin to do any of them. It's when we allow things and situations to begin to rule our life, dominating our time. I was trading one addiction for another. I never fully overcame my sexual struggles, I only found a way for one to compliment the other. To blend them together masked the appearance of destruction. Alcohol would either numb the pain of me feeling worthless in a spiritual sense, even though in the physical, it made me feel like I was accepted. I was feeling ten-foot-tall and bulletproof. I would push the boundaries by what I would say, the way, or the tone of my voice. I was insinuating, compromising, and provocative.

The physical intimacy from another woman didn't matter I wasn't wanting intimacy or a relationship. Yes, I very much enjoyed sex with my wife. But now, now I enjoy true intimacy with her more than ever. Call it a spark, a connection I don't know. It's as if I see my wife in a new light with new eyes, and our physical intimacy means so much more than just sex, now. It was the thrill of the chase, being in pursuit of, seeing just how far I could push the limits without being caught. I was seeing how far I could get or what I could get away with. These were all under the cover of alcohol consumption as I continued to feed my sexual desires.

It wasn't until I recognized my struggle with pornography and sexual tenancies as an addiction. Addictions can be demons that take hold of our life and our desires, and they consume us. We feel the feelings of guilt, shame, ridicule, confusion, condemnation, feeling unworthy, lies, and deceit. As we give in to temptations, we feed those demons and they grow stronger. They will not be satisfied until they have taken complete control of our life. I believe their ultimate satisfaction comes when they have destroyed every ounce of good within a person. All too often that destruction will spread to the one's that love and care about us.

It's only by allowing the light of God to shine into our life. Every dark corner and hidden closet of our life must be exposed. We should leave no place for those demons to hide. We should be allowing the Spirit of God to consume us to the point it flows out to others.

> For you were once darkness, but now you are light in the Lord. Live as children of light (for the fruit of the light consists in all goodness, righteousness, and truth) and find out what pleases the Lord. Have nothing to do with the fruitless deeds of darkness, but rather expose them. (Eph. 5:8–11, NIV)

> You prepare a table before me in the presence of my enemies. You anoint my

head with oil; my cup over-
flows. (Ps. 23:5, NIV)

Does your life overflow with goodness, righteousness, and truth? These are found only in God, our heavenly Father, by accepting Jesus Christ as our Lord and Savior, allowing the Holy Spirit to lead, guide, and direct our life!

If you haven't already, isn't it time that you to draw a line? You need stop feeding your demons. You should allow the light of God to shine into your life. Accept Jesus as your Lord and Savior! Then find someone you can trust and make yourself accountable to them.

We continued our life, doing what made us feel happy. Wait, I want to back up in that statement, I continued to drag Lisa along as I pursued to find some form of happiness.

Even though I made a lot of insinuations, I never had physically followed thru with them. Well, except for that one time and Lisa didn't know about that anyway. Still, in Lisa's eyes, I had cheated on her, and more than once. The trust had been broken, and I had stomped on her heart, destroying even a trace of trust. As she was constantly questioning where I was going, where I had been, what I was doing, and why was I getting home from work later than normal, it still hadn't sunk into my head how badly I had hurt her. Yeah, I loved her, why wasn't that enough?

Seriously, what's the harm's in me looking at another woman that's dressed, how can I say what I want to and be politically correct? I'm not sure I can be politically correct. A little on the trashy side, provocative, sexually arousing or seductively dressed does the wording really matter? When a woman is dressed in tight clothes, low cut tops, short shorts, see-through material, maybe it's just the way they move when they walk or dance. It's obvious, in my mind they desire attention, and a guy's going to notice certain things, especially when it feeds his addiction.

I didn't get how Lisa felt that I didn't value her or how I had cheapened our relationship. Just because she wouldn't dress that way surely didn't mean that I couldn't look when I saw something that I found intriguing. After all, I loved her, I worked hard so she didn't have to. Why should she deny me of looking at or watching another woman?

What's going on in my mind wasn't hurting anyone.

Still, we had multiple fights over my being so secretive or I'd get caught looking just a little too long. Why not look? After all, I wasn't sleeping with anyone else, I wasn't chatting with anyone but her. Never mind the fact that she felt that I had. It's a wonder we stayed together. I honestly believe if her parents weren't some three thousand miles away, I know she would have left me.

There were times it felt like a rage within—all the guilt and shame that was bottled up. I know there were a lot of times that I closed everyone off, angry words would push Lisa away. Even though, in my heart, I didn't mean them. Why did I do and say most of the things I did? Who am I? Later, everything was fine, only the pain from my words increased the doubt and mistrust in Lisa.

It was New Year's Eve, and our group went out to celebrate. Really, it was just another excuse to party on!

One of the guys had a single "female" cousin that came out with us that evening. Maybe there was a subconscious thought deep in my mind. She wasn't all that attractive, and she wasn't there to chase a man. In a way, I think that I felt sorry for her. During the course of the night, I had danced several dances with her. Never once did I get out of line. I was the perfect gentleman. After all, she was my friend's cousin. The same friend whose wife was my wife's best friend. I knew to even try something wouldn't end well, so I didn't.

We all drank, danced, and had a good time that night. The problem was that I had drank enough that I didn't realize it was the last dance of the night, which I danced with her instead of my wife. Big mistake, I heard about that the entire ride home, along with all the questions about the night. What had I done? Did we sneak off? Did we have fun? Did we go somewhere and fool around? Maybe we had gone off and had sex? Maybe I would like to go home with her? Are you beginning to get the picture?

Now it was about a fifteen to twenty-minute ride home, and Lisa was still going off about the night. I had tried to explain that nothing had happened! I honestly didn't realize that was the last song! I knew I had been guilty of hiding things in my past, but come on. I knew that Lisa wasn't trusting. I had asked her if it was okay to dance with her. Lisa had seemed okay with things during the night.

She was convinced it was because I was trying to get this gal to sleep with me—whether it was that night or sometime in the near future. Maybe for the first time in a long time, I was being honest. I really and truly didn't realize it was going to be the last song. I had been a gentleman, keeping my hands to myself. We hadn't snuck off, we hadn't kissed, and I didn't even attempt to steal a kiss. Nothing!

The barrage of accusations continued as rage began to swell up deep within me. I was sorry about not dancing that last dance with Lisa. "I didn't do anything." All the times I had lied, but this time, I wasn't, and Lisa wouldn't believe me. I was being honest with her, all but begging her to stop with the accusations.

I'm not proud of what happened next, I wanted to physically hit her to make her shut up. Instead, I slammed her up against the wall rather than hitting her, (What's the difference?) then I literally picked her up and threw her on our bed. She wouldn't listen, she wouldn't stop with the accusations, all the noise in my head. "I didn't do anything wrong!" With my hands around her throat, I stopped even though I was still in a rage, only now I was angry that I had lost control. I was feeling angry and ashamed that I had physically hurt Lisa like that.

Between everything that happened that night, I had lost complete respect from Lisa. She had every right to call the police and press charges. It didn't matter how sorry I was. I had crossed a line that night. I viewed it as "her" fault because "she" didn't believe me. If "she" would have just stopped with all "her" questions. Honestly; if the roles had been reversed, I wouldn't have believed me either.

As I gathered my composure, I decided that it wasn't going to ever matter what I did or didn't do. Lisa wasn't going to *ever* believe anything that I ever said, so if there was a next time, I may as well push the limits and see what happens.

Rebuilding

On May 22, 2011, our lives changed. In fact, it changed an entire town and everyone that lived there. I was working nights that weekend, and as I left the house, Lisa was considering mowing our yard. About the time I got to work, the tornado sirens went off. Someone said a tornado was four miles to the north of us. I knew if that was the case, we'd be fine. I still called Lisa just to check on her and let her know where I heard it was. She said the sky was clear, and that she was okay.

For safety reasons, they had us in the storm shelter at work till we were given the all-clear. It was about twenty minutes later when the plant operations manager came by the plant to make sure everything and everyone was okay. As I was talking with him, he said a big home supply store had been leveled.

"That's less than a mile from our house!" I said. His next words were "GO!"

Due to trees and debris blocking the roads, the closets I was able to get to our house was about a mile. I parked my car and set out for home on foot. As I jogged the path of destruction, complete businesses—*gone*, homes—*gone*. I couldn't get ahold of Lisa as the cell services were down. My mind raced with questions—what was I going to find? Was Lisa okay? Did we even still have a home? Our car? Our pets? As I turned on our street, wait, is this our street? Nothing looked the same, I had to climb over a huge tree, laying across the road. Once on the other side, I had hope. I could see houses still standing.

We took about $40,000 in damages and lost our Jeep Wrangler. Lisa was in a state of shock, but she was okay! Our two dogs were also fine.

Then, my second concern kicked in, our daughter and her family only lived six blocks away toward the center of the mile-wide path of destruction that the tornado had left. Lisa had somehow already walked over and checked on them.

They had ridden the storm out in their bathroom. Bethany and the two girls had stayed in the bathtub while her husband was sitting on the floor with his back against the tub and his feet holding the door closed. It was nothing short of a miracle as their home was destroyed, but they didn't have a scratch one on them.

I turned my attention back to Lisa, asking where she was at when the tornado hit. Now we have never been one to get worked up and take shelter when there was a threat of a tornado. For some reason, that day she had taken our two dogs and went to our bathroom, which is in the center of our house. This was *totally* out of character for her since normally, she would have just sat in our living room. While we didn't take a direct hit, the twelve-foot picture window in our living room blew in. sending little slivers of glass all throughout our living room/dining room.

Lisa's chair, where she would normally be sitting, was full of glass. Had she been sitting there, if she would have even survived, odds are extremely high that she would be blind. For a change, I did recognize that my family had been blessed. God had protected through the storm in the most literal sense. It just didn't mean that I was going to change my ways. Some would say it was because of my guilt, shame, and feelings of being unworthy. I had embraced my anger of so-called Christians and they're better than thou attitudes.

How many times had I prayed to overcome my failures and my shortcomings? It had been one big vicious circle that I could never quite rise above. If there was a God, He evidently didn't want me. I had accepted all these lies, "Hell will freeze over before I set foot in a church again!"

As our neighborhood began the rebuilding process, our homes were the top priority. The people in our neighborhood became close, developing good friendships. Everyone was willing to help each other. There were a lot of people that came from all over the United States to help, different churches and organizations. Needless to say, that was a long, hard summer.

Despite everything, my struggles continued, masked behind our going out to the casinos every chance we got. I still was in it for me, determined to find something that would satisfy my inner most desires, calming the rage.

Lisa and I became really good friends with a widow lady down the street. I'm not sure just what all Lisa had shared with her. I just know that she was never judgmental of me. She was certainly persistent, and about every three or four months, she would drop the most subtle of hints, inviting us to church. I wasn't going to be hateful or disrespectful, she was nothing but kind to us. Never once was she in my face about my drinking or my language, and never once did she tell me that I was on the fast track to hell. My response was generally about the same every time, "Hell will have to freeze over before I ever set foot in a church again!!"

Sure, on more than one occasion we had a conversation about church. I didn't mix words as I shared how I felt that Christians are all judgmental hypocrites. Well, at least 95 percent of them, and I didn't need any more of that in my life. I can be a good person without church, not that I even considered myself a good person at that point in my life.

Her response was that we're all sinners saved only by the grace of God. Every one of us slips throughout a day. Who was I kidding? It wasn't "those people" holding me back or standing between myself and God. I mean the doors swing both ways. I just didn't want to take the responsibility for me, my actions, and *my selfishness*. It was easier to put the blame on anyone else other than myself. It's their fault, after all, they're the ones professing holiness.

With everything that I had done and all that I had put Lisa through during all our years together I still loved her, even if it didn't appear that I did. I *never* meant to hurt her, although time and time again, I stomped her heart, crushing her spirit. While Lisa, even to this day, refuses to be called a victim, truth is she was a victim, my victim. She just refuses to play the part allowing pity or brokenness to have reign in her life.

I still hadn't got to that point of really wanting to change. I was only disappointed and sorry that I would get caught looking at or talking to an unfamiliar female! It was as if she knew my thoughts, my desires, and what I might do if given the chance. My desires, my needs, my feelings, and needing to feel good about myself, *me*—it was still all about *me*! Why couldn't Lisa comprehend that? Why wouldn't she just cater to my wants, needs, and desires? If she would only understand that, everything would be so much better. If she would just do what I wanted and let me do whatever I wanted.

Today, I reflect on my writing and on my life, even as recent as this very day that I write these words. "Not even a hint" came to mind as Lisa reminded me of those very words. See, a couple of days, ago we were at a "church family" event where I was talking with another woman. Now I try to be cautious, never alone or in a comprising situation with another woman, especially a single woman. I had survived the situation and our surroundings. I had thought that as we were standing near other people, close enough that anyone could hear our conversation. It was okay. I suppose I really didn't give it enough thought. I can honestly say that I didn't have any of those old feelings of lust and perversion that I use to have.

However, it was afterward when I walked up to Lisa, that look on her face, I knew what she was thinking. Later, she questioned the conversation, my thoughts during the conversation, instantly assuming that I was slipping back into my old ways.

Still again, today, Lisa brought all this up as it resembled the actions of my past. I wish that I could write about how I managed this conversation in a Godly manner, I fear that I failed. No matter how good my intentions may have been, I had left "a hint" of doubt in Lisa's mind, something I just can't do now. While God forgives and forgets, that's not our human nature, hard as we may try.

When you hurt someone like I did, you have to walk a very tight rope with little to no margin of era. Every action or reaction counts for something.

If you want to rebuild your relationship, you're going to have to answer the hard questions and not leave room for doubt. Without realizing, I had let my guard down, and Satan hit Lisa with thoughts of doubt and insecurity. Satan, at his best, in an attempt to divide and conquer, had placed doubt in Lisa's mind while stirring up a wave of anger within me that would draw both of us off our focus of Christ.

> Be alert and of sober mind. Your enemy the devil prowls around like a roaring lion looking for someone to devour. (1 Peter 5:8, NIV)

Anger is the trigger that can set off any number of sinful actions. If we will understand and recognize those triggers, we can get ahead of our struggles. Follow this example and see if you've ever been down this road.

Jesus spoke about not looking at a woman and lusting.

> But I tell you that anyone who looks at a woman lustfully has already committed adultery with her in his heart. (Matthew 5:28, NIV)

Now if you back up a few verses, you find He speaks about anger.

> But I tell you that anyone who is angry with a brother or sister, will be subject to judgment. Again, anyone

> who says to a brother or sister, 'Raca,' is answerable to the court. And anyone who says, 'You fool!' will be in danger of the fire of hell. (Matt. 5:22, NIV)

Don't you find it interesting that Paul said to not let the sun go down while you are angry?

> In your anger do not sin: Do not let the sun go down while you are still angry. (Eph. 4:26; Matt. 5:22, NIV)

Since more often than not, illicit behaviors occur at night under the cover of the darkness.

Now compare it to your own life. Has there ever been a time that you wanted to have sex and your spouse said no? Did you have feelings of disappointment and anger? Oh sure maybe we said it was fine, but we really were "in the mood." Did you have the attitude of "fine," as your spouse goes to bed?

OUR STRUGGLES ARE REAL!

The house is quiet as you begin to surf the internet. Maybe you check out a chat line, or you just browse through multiple profiles in search of the one. Perhaps you didn't even plan on doing any more than just "looking." Until you seen the one, OH you know the one. They have that certain intriguing and seductive look that you just can't resist.

See how our anger/disappointment triggered a reaction. Understanding our triggers play a large part in living a victorious Christian life—this is one of the hardest lessons for me to learn and I'm still working on it. Even when I don't feel those old pressures or desires, I must guard against the very appearance, remembering "not even a hint."

You may remember the question "WWJD," what would Jesus do? While that is still a good question for us to ask ourselves, I want to suggest another question for those of us that are in a relationship, "WWMST," what would my spouse think?

> Husbands, love your wives, just as Christ loved the church and gave himself up for her. (Eph. 5:25, NIV)

If we truly love our spouse, we're going to at least attempt to make them feel safe and secure. We should be willing to give up ourselves for them. We need to care about their physical, mental, emotional and spiritual health. As the husband, we should also desire that our wife is received into heaven—as we have become as one that is part of our responsibility too.

Therefore, we should care about what they think and how our actions make them feel. After all, if they have been around for any length of time. Our wife may know us better than we know ourselves, which means they know our addictions. There is a lot of truth in the statement, "Once an addict always an addict!" Facing our demons together, as there is strength in numbers.

> Therefore confess your sins to each other and pray for each other so that you may be healed. The prayer of a righteous person is powerful and effective. (James 5:16, NIV)

OUR STRUGGLES ARE REAL!

The biggest challenge is getting other guys to admit that they too have these same struggles. Becoming vulnerable, accountable, and transparent goes against our male ego. Allowing ourselves to show weakness means we must lay aside our pride. It has become easy for me to share with other guys. Maybe because I understand what it was like to not have anyone that I could confide in and trust. I know how important it is to not betray that trust. Or that I know when we open up we can find freedom. However, even when I'm going through my own personal struggles, I hate to show that weakness to Lisa. I want her to feel secure, safe, and valued. This in itself is a good reason why it's beneficial to have someone to talk with. I also believe it's good to have multiple accountability partners, two or three if possible. Not everyone can be available 100 percent of the time.

Please don't misunderstand me, I'm not saying that a husband and wife aren't accountable to each other, because they are.

You need a circle of friends (of the same sex) that will listen, and not always agreeing with you. A friend that's not there, trying to fix you, heal you, save you, or correct you.

There are times we just need a friend without advice, solutions, or the next steps. They don't have to have the answer to our life's problems and they don't even have to act like they do. Sometimes, we just need that friend who can show up and just be there as you process life and your struggles.

Sometimes, we need a friend that will share their struggles and how they overcome their issues—not as a solution for us, but a guidance and hope. We need someone that will challenge you, not just holding you to a standard of purity. Someone who will help you discover those triggers, the little things that set us off. Accountability partners need to know when to speak and when to just listen.

Cut Out and Moving On

Even in all of our party life, Lisa and I had made friends with a couple around my mom's age. This lady had gotten to know us before putting together what family I was from. It turned out that growing up, she and my mom were really good friends. This lady recognized what a gem Lisa was, she absolutely adored Lisa. This lady made several attempts to help reunite us with my mother.

It just wasn't meant to be. The lady felt that it was a real shame that my mother had never really gotten to know Lisa. Making the comment that she would have loved to have Lisa for her daughter or daughter-in-law.

It was a couple of years after rebuilding from the tornado that we learned that my mother had passed away. Maybe it was guilt or perhaps I just felt obliged to return home. I didn't like some of the things that had happened since we stopped going around. But mom had made it clear that we weren't welcome.

There had been several people that had helped themselves to things that were my mother's, including money, *all* in the name of helping her. There's not much to share about that chapter of my life. In my parents' eyes, I wasn't an obedient or deserving son, willing to follow and do everything that they wanted. As my final punishment, even from their grave, I found myself cut out of any inheritance, which was fine. I know down in my heart the only way I would have ever been able to appease my mother, to even begin to get back in her good graces, would have been to forsake Lisa by divorcing her.

Now I know that I have hurt Lisa beyond measure. And in my heart, in my own way, I have always loved her, never wanting to hurt her. I will always believe that God brought us together and it has only been by His good grace that has kept us together.

My issue was the fact that my dad's half brother had cleaned everything out. While there were provisions for our kids, my parents' grandchildren, he had taken everything. Only proving that money may very well be the root of evil.

Our lives continued, and we've relied on no one down through our years. Maybe that has played a part in my lack of faith in God as a father. Have you ever found yourself comparing God, our heavenly father, with your earthly father? If you have been abused or neglected by your father, we tend to associate one with the other. Because that's what we know and understand, its how we relate.

We've always struggled, but we've always had enough to take care of our family. We've never had extravagant or exotic vacations, but we gave our kids a stable home and some decent vacations. In part, that was Lisa's reasoning for not bringing my struggles and issues to light, all to protect Richard and Bethany from my twisted and perverted desires of life since she didn't want our kids to lose their love and respect for me. Even though she's struggled with feelings of being unwanted, unworthy, unattractive, and simply not wanted or loved, all these issues were only compounded by the rejection from the man she had loved, who's children she bore. What had happened to the guy she fell in love with and married?

She had the feeling that she wasn't enough or somehow she wasn't the woman that her man wanted or even desired. All these feelings and emotions had installed a deep sense of simply *not* being good enough.

Down through all our years together, Lisa has constantly been totally selfless while all I've been was consistently selfish.

As I reflect back, it truly pains me not having that many good memories. Why is it that we always remember the bad times? Has life been so consumed by my selfish desires that I have stumbled through it, never really living it? Neglecting having a relationship with those that I love, only to go to work, putting in long hours to buy them things. Was it to provide for them or provide them with the things they wanted in an attempt to buy their love?

Our lives returned to somewhat normal, however, our little bike group slowly broke up. Once again, it was back to just Lisa and me, which was probably a good thing. Our going out, going to bike events, all tapered off, it just wasn't the same as it was going out with a group.

We were more family-focused, both of our kids were married, and we had grandchildren now. Four little girls to light up our lives, two from each of our kids.

I've purposely stayed away from sharing their lives while writing this, they have their story—even though our lives are so intertwined with our children and our granddaughters. Now I've explained how I have always felt my parents attempted to be overruling and controlling in our life. That in itself caused me to want to be different, and we've always been there for our kids. I don't believe that we have ever tried to "run" their lives. Good choices or bad ones, we've always been there for them, offering whatever guidance or counsel we could, standing behind them along the way. Hard as it's been, we've watched them fall at times. But we have always been there to help them get back up.

I do feel in order to keep our connection, you, the reader, and me, you need to know just a few more things. Both our kids have been through a divorce, Bethany's was relatively simple because there were no children involved. Richard's divorce, on the other hand, has been a total nightmare. As much as we love those girls, there have been times we felt upset because we felt more like the parents, robbed of being their grandparents. But the blessings we've had because of our time with them has far outweighed it all. We have watched each one of them develop their own personalities. It brings joy as we watch their faith in God develop, teaching them how and listening as they pray. Grandchildren are a way to maybe get it right. Thank you Lord for second chances?

For several years, our vacations and even most day or weekend trips were made on the bike. I laugh and joke that I burned Lisa out on going on the bike all the time. Sure, I had a bit of a wild streak. I enjoyed the speed and curves on two wheels, and I still do. However, I believe the biggest thing that quenched her riding desires were those little girls—especially Richard's girls. They so needed some stability in their lives since divorce can be so messy. I guess I was still hanging on to some of my own selfishness as I didn't get that for a long time.

Sure, she said that I could go by myself, and maybe I would have. But I didn't, maybe there was a part of me that was afraid of what I might do if Lisa wasn't around at all. If I was given the opportunity to have some other chick on the back of my bike with me, what would I do? For Lisa to not go just didn't seem right. However, my other thoughts about possible options wouldn't be right either. I would rather give up riding than risk doing something that could very well cost me everything. I loved my wife despite my actions. I didn't want to lose her, and I had came so close so many times.

Sure, I still struggled, maybe not as much. Unfortunately, I had discovered a local ad page that had, shall we say, "women available." Now it wasn't phone sex, it was more along the lines of for $$, they would do whatever you would like for them to do. It was a way that I could develop my own fantasy with someone that was real.

As I wasn't willing to pay for sex, I would call to find out any particulars that they would be willing to disclose over the phone. Then knowing what they would be willing to do, I could create my own fantasy and relieve my stress while I was in the shower. After all, I've never been past self-gratification! It had a certain amount of thrill in the chase just to see what type of acts they would be willing to engage in.

The biggest problem was that it gave them a link back to me through either e-mail, messenger, or phone. I guess sometimes they knew that guys were just wasting their time, poking around. I think it was their way of getting back at the guys that did that, to send random messages. It wasn't so fun if and when Lisa would see messages, insinuating that I was to meet someone, somewhere.

I remember one such message, "Let's meet at the fifteenth street bookstore. I'm clean!" Yeah, Lisa saw that, and I had a ton of questions to answer. The problem was I honestly didn't know who it was, what they were thinking, or if it was even legitimate! I must admit that to read the message sounded like I had something planned. I think the kicker for Lisa was the fact there actually was a bookstore on fifteenth street that we had even been in before. Sure, I had an idea of what was going on, but I hadn't set anything up. I'd been set up all right, *but* I sure wasn't going to admit to what I had been dabbling in.

Flat on my Back

It's now 2016, I began to notice, depending on how I was sitting in a chair, my right butt cheek had a tendency to go numb. I just brush it off, like it was no big deal, I probably was just sitting wrong and it was "going to sleep." Even though it was becoming more and more frequent, I tried the chiropractic thing, seeking to find some relief.

I remember it was on a Monday because it was the day after mother's day, I was hurting. I had a pain in my lower back down into my butt, I could barely sit in the passenger seat as I rode to the store with Lisa. Looking at me and the way I was sitting, she asked if I needed to go to the doctor. Now I really don't like to go to the doctor, even though we have insurance, I just don't usually go. But my answer that morning was yes!

From our family doctor to an orthopedic doctor, having an MRI done, having the spinal shot to physical therapy. The hoops one must jump through even with insurance. Nothing seemed to help relieve the pain, I couldn't even sit up. My physical therapist cut me loose at 7:50 a.m. on a Friday because therapy wasn't doing any good. I was back in to see our family doctor by 9:30 a.m., and by noon, I was leaving the orthopedic doctor's office with a pending surgery date.

I guess I've been fortunate because I had never had a major surgery before. But to resolve this issue meant surgery, as I had a herniated disk, pinching my Sciatica nerve. By the morning of my surgery, the numbness had traveled down my left leg, causing me to lose most of the feeling from my butt to my toes. I couldn't even wiggle my toes, now that was a scary feeling.

Now I'm sure you know what a pain it can be to make a doctor's appointment. So many times, you try to schedule an appointment and it's always two or three days later. Yet that day, appointments were made and kept within a few hours, that's like unheard of! I wasn't living right with God at that time. But I have to question how did all those morning events fall into place if it wasn't for a higher power of authority?

I had a lot of time to think, thirteen weeks I was off work. The one big question that kept going through my mind was; What if I couldn't ever work again? And what about Lisa? She had to do everything inside our house and out. The one thing that I wasn't going to do was lay there and make promises to God, that more than likely I wouldn't keep anyway.

> When you make a vow to God, do not delay to fulfill it. He has no pleasure in fools; fulfill your vow. (Eccles. 5:4, NIV)

I wouldn't say that I was angry with God at the time. Why should I be? I hadn't been living a life that was even remotely pleasing to *him*. I was just living *my* life to please me.

Now during the summer months, our son's two girls usually spend most of their time with us. I think that was the first time those girls saw Papa cry. The pain of not being able to stand and walk, having to belly crawl one day just to get into the house.

Lisa and one of the girls had gone for a walk one morning when the doorbell sounded. I managed to go to the door, only to discover it was one of the neighbor ladies. Apparently, she had talked to our one friend, you remember, the one that kept inviting me to church. She had come down to check on and pray for me. Even then, I barely let her in the door. My one granddaughter was there, so it really wasn't an issue. She asked if she could pray for me, well, what could I say, other than "sure." I figured it would be easier to just let her pray so she'd leave.

See, it wasn't the prayer that got my attention. She finished praying, and as she turned to leave, she handed me a folded check, which I was refused to take. She explained that she and her husband felt led to give it to us. How if I refused to accept the check, it would be robbing a blessing from them. I'd heard that pitch before, so I reluctantly took the check, politely thanking her and laid it on the entertainment center, not even looking at the amount it was written for.

Of course, when Lisa got home, our granddaughter was telling her about the lady coming down and how she had prayed for Papa. As I told Lisa who it was that had come down, she asked me if I had been "*nice*." She knew how I felt about church people. "Yeah, I was, and before she would leave, she gave us this." I handed Lisa the folded check. The amount was $5, less than our house payment. Of course, Lisa went down to talk with her and thanked her, making sure they were okay being so generous. Within $5 of our house payment, that's no "pitch."

The point is, even though I wasn't living a God-fearing life, He had spoken in a very real and tangible manner that morning. Some of the walls in my life had at least started to crack.

I was out of work for thirteen weeks. Financially, we were hurting, but somehow we were always able to pay our house payments and our utilities, never missing a meal.

I had asked about physical therapy during my recovery, the doctor only suggested that I walk, nothing specific. He explained how a person can simply step off the curb onto the street and throw out their back. Hey, he's the doctor, who was I to question him?

As I was released from his care and returned back to work, my attitude was different. I think that I was more thankful for being able to work and provide for my family. Even though I knew that physically. I wasn't able to be the workhorse that I had always been. I had learned a new word when asked to work extra, "No."

Sure, I could use the extra money, who can't? It was in part because I had always been willing to work any time they needed an extra man. I grew up being taught that if you work hard, you can move on up in a company. That didn't seem the case—you work hard, you do what your asked, and you do it well. It's the guy that's related to someone higher up or the one that only tells the bosses what they want to hear. So much for "honesty and integrity" in the workforce. Tell them what's not right, what needs to be fixed, and be persistent to make things right or at least better. You are deemed just hard to get along with. Promote the favorite, and I didn't stand a chance. I continued to do my job to the best of my abilities even if others were slacking, at least in my opinion.

As our life was once again returning back to somewhat normal, Lisa made a decision. She had decided it was time for her to get back in church, leaving me the option to do whatever I felt I needed to do. To be really honest, I knew she was right, however, I felt set-up. We always did things together, maybe our lives would have been different if we had some kind of productive hobbies separate from each other. But we didn't, I wasn't just going to sit at home while she went, even if it was going to church. Then there was the issue of where to go. The thoughts going through Lisa's mind was where would I be accepted with my tattoos.

Oh, my bad, last I mentioned about tattoos was when I had the one done on my right forearm. Seems I failed to write about the countless hours I spent in a tattoo shop. This time it had begun with a wolf on my left shoulder blade and we'll leave it at the fact ink tends to run. Let's just say that I was fortunate to become good friends with a couple of tattoo artists. Because financially I would never have been able to afford the amount of work I've had done, there was a lot that I was able to trade out with my woodworking skills.

If I learned anything during that time, "those people" that I use to call freaks, they're just like you and me on the inside. I learned to not be so quick to judge because someone's different. That doesn't mean we have to agree with them or even like the way they choose to express themselves. Now I had become one of them.

Depending on church people's reactions, that could very well determine my spiritual outcome.

Evidently, hell got a little frosty one Sunday morning in August, as we went to our neighbor's church, I was more uncomfortable than the people there. Everyone was welcoming and friendly, the music was okay, and the word was strong. We continued to attend there on Sundays.

Church had changed from when I grew up, now they only having one service a week. Sure, you may have several options as far as times, which worked out for my schedule. I guess that's the whole point, to try to make it possible for everyone to at least be able to attend. In the back of my mind, I figured this church was large enough that I could go, which would make Lisa happy. That I would be able to get lost in the crowd of people, come and go with no real connections.

Something that they did that was different for me was their way of doing communion, taking it on the first Sunday of every month. Now the way that I grew up, it was taught that you didn't take communion unless you had accepted Christ as your Lord and Savior.

> So then, whoever eats the bread or drinks the cup of the Lord in an unworthy manner will be guilty of sinning against the body and blood of the Lord.
> Everyone ought to examine themselves before they eat of the bread and drink from the cup. (1 Cor. 11:27–28, NIV)

So with that thought, there was no way that I was taking communion. I knew I wasn't living a life that was pleasing to God. The next month on that first Sunday, I found a reason to not attend, but I still knew I wasn't living right, and I sure wasn't going to take communion. I felt the conviction of the Holy Spirit in my life. I knew it was time to either be all in or out, and the out hadn't been working so well for me.

By the next communion, I had asked God for the forgiveness of my sins, making things right between Him and I. Now I'm not saying that I didn't still have my sexual struggles. I had given my life back to Jesus. I still wasn't sure how active I really wanted to be in church. My intent had been to just blend in. Now as I had accepted Jesus as my Lord and Savior, everything was changing. I've never been able to just sit on the sidelines and not engage.

Before I knew it, we were attending Sunday school and church on Sunday mornings and small groups on Wednesday evenings. Lisa attended regularly while my attendance was only as my work schedule would allow. Still, I was able to attend three out of four weeks.

Our quality of life was improving, and once again, God was included in it. I still was a master of secrecy as I continued to flirt with sexual options, providing a variety of fantasies. Still, I was wrapped up in my selfishness, *but* I was appeasing Lisa. I didn't want to lose her. I couldn't lose her. Despite my failures in our marriage, she was the one constant. I loved her with all my heart, and I still do! She has always been the example of true love in my life. Never manipulating or controlling with alternative motives.

I know there were times we argued, times we strongly disagreed, and times I used my anger at Lisa to justify my illicit behavior. No matter what or how I achieved my pleasure, to obtain my sexual release, I always hated myself afterward, feeling the battle of right and wrong raging within. This was then followed by a tidal wave of guilt, shame, and being unworthy. I was nothing more than a *failure*! Time after time, as my behavior constantly repeated for over forty years, I hated myself and who I had become, especially since I knew better, morally and spiritually. So much failure in my life, as a man, husband, and father.

Why? Why do I constantly fail God? Why do I fail Lisa? Why do I tear at the emotions of the one person, that would have given me the world if she could? There were times that I honestly thought my death would certainly be a remedy and that Lisa would be better off without me. It was only the fear of God that I didn't try to hurt myself.

Despite how easy it would be to throw in the towel to our marriage, I knew our marriage was ordained by God. He brought Lisa and me together! Despite all the destruction and pain I've caused, God has kept us together somehow. The one thing that I could tangibly hold onto has been our marriage and Lisa. The two things that I will fight for till my last breath. Christ first with Lisa and our life together next.

> Husbands, in the same way be considerate as you live with your wives, and treat them with respect as the weaker partner and as heirs with you of the gracious gift of life, so that nothing will hinder your prayers. (1 Peter 3:7, NIV)

OUR STRUGGLES ARE REAL!

Yeah, I had totally crashed and burned on that one. The phrase, "Stomped a mudhole in it," comes to mind. Maybe this time could be different.

Rock Bottom Low

I had been back to work for thirteen weeks when I was moving a large roll (6'x36"), pushing it forward into position when I strained my back. I felt it, and I knew something just didn't feel right. This was a new pain and it wasn't going away. I followed the incident/accident procedures at work, which included a trip to the E.R. A long story short, I had reinjured my back again. Thankfully, the pain level wasn't nearly as bad as before. This pain was more of a constant discomfort in my back.

For the next ten weeks, I had physical therapy, strengthening my core and my back. While we were serving God, well Lisa was, I really was just attempting to live a Christ-like life. I still wasn't really focused on Him. I had the time, but I wasn't getting in the Word or spending time in prayer like I needed to. Not if I was going to build a genuine relationship with Him.

I was concerned about our bills and surviving yet another setback. The workman's compensation insurance challenged the accident as being a preexisting condition. There were tests and hoops I had to go through. But in the end, it was proven to be a new injury, which in a way was a small miracle in itself. At least there would be some money coming in.

It was the first part of January before I was released from doctor's care and was able to return back to work. My doctor had voiced his concern about my job duties. According to him, he had been on a safety advisory team that had previously determined a certain level of hazards at the location of my incident. They had made recommendations, which obviously was NOT followed.

While my doctor's comments were troubling and I had my concerns about my job, I had to provide for Lisa and I. Like everyone else we had bills to pay and we hadn't fully recovered from me being off the first time. When everything was going good, I made fairly decent money, so we enjoyed spoiling our granddaughters. Plus we did or bought what we wanted without much thought.

Things at work were different this time as I returned to work. My hopes that maybe I could advance to a higher position were shattered. If anything, management made several attempts to get me to say that I wasn't able to perform my regular job duties. I had seen them do this to people before. I knew if I said anything even remotely close to that I couldn't do my job, they would find a reason, and I'd be gone. Almost twenty-two years of service really didn't mean anything. I felt their constant questioning, borderline harassment, even though I didn't push that issue. I continued to do my job only now it seemed like I was just going through the motions.

While I was disappointed in some areas in my life, despite my personnel struggles, I was slowly becoming more involved in our church. We had even joined becoming members, committing to be regular, helping out wherever and whenever we could. We had found our church home. and it was becoming more like belonging to a family than anywhere we had ever attended.

During that eight-nine-month period, while I had my back issues, my sexual struggles weren't a priority. After all, when you're in pain, lying flat on your back, some things lose their luster.

How sad and pathetic we humans can be, going from needing God in one moment to not even recognizing who God is in the next. In a matter of a few seconds, we forget so quickly! As we attempt to serve God we hear other Christians talking about God's grace. How we are saved by grace and how because of grace it's no big deal if we fail, we have God's grace. Even though I was trying to straddle a fence, their definition of how grace works sounded more like abusing God's grace to me. But maybe I could use the grace of God this way in my own life. What if I had been wrong in my understanding? After all, the way I had been going I was consistently failing. Could it be that's what grace is? Could that be how grace works? It sure would be a lot easier to just do what I wanted, when I wanted and attend church claiming grace. That would be the best of both worlds!

I began to wonder what if all those times of me feeling like a failure had just been life's natural course. It sounded good, I could live my life the way I wanted, church on Sunday mornings, small groups on Wednesdays, and no more struggling. If I mess up or fail, oh well! After all I have God's grace to fall back on. However, if that's the case why do we need grace to help, if it does in fact cover? The apostle Paul wrote,

> Let us then approach God's throne of grace with confidence, so that we may receive mercy and find grace to help us in our time of need. (Hebrews 4:16, NIV)

If grace covers anything and everything that we choose to do, why did Jesus say;

> Enter through the narrow gate. For wide is the gate and broad is the road that leads to destruction, and many enter through it. But small is the gate and narrow the road that leads to life, and only a few

find it. (Matthew 7:13–14, NIV)

Narrow doesn't sound like anything and everything!

I knew in my heart there is right and wrong, and there's no straddling a fence. Grace is there for us when we stumbled NOT so we can sin!

Still, I was so weary of the constant struggle to do what seemed right. For the next six months, I continued down the same path that I had for years. I was being more secretive and cautious all the while continuing to flirt with the prospect of having some type of erotic sexual experience. I still desired to have the ultimate sexual encounter of some form, attempting to find complete and total satisfaction and pleasure. To find my own sexual utopia would be fulfilling and somehow make me and my life complete.

The solo self-satisfaction, self-gratification of my masturbation was getting old—they no longer were quite enough. I needed something physical with another woman getting me off. I want you to understand that at no time in my married life did Lisa withhold sex from me or use it as a means of manipulation. The fact is, early on in our marriage I force or at least she felt forced at times to have sex with me. For years I thought that I had to have sex so I could sleep at night! Then later, she felt that if she didn't have sex with me, I might do who knows what. I had to have that sexual encounter, achieving my release!

I know that I've stated this probably multiple times, I want you to completely understand how I felt all those years. There was such a driving desire, a raging storm deep inside of me. While I've never had issues with drugs, I can only imagine that my inner feelings, that driving desire, or need for a "fix" are much the same type of feelings that I experienced.

My fantasies, all the perverted thoughts that had run through my head, had twisted my perception. Lisa had established moral values in her life that she wasn't willing to cross. It had always been me that wanted more "adventure." Someone like all the women in the adult movies, uninhibited. It wasn't like I hadn't made multiple twisted suggestions about various sexual acts to Lisa.

After all, when you see it on the screen, it must be real, right? The perception of sexual bliss and complete satisfaction distorted by my selfish desires and what I want to believe. There had been several times when I made sexual suggestions that her response was, I could get someone else who would do that. What she had meant to be a definite *no*. I turn into permission being given. Remember, it's all in how you play the words.

It had been long enough since I had experienced sex with someone other than my wife that the desire once again began to burn. That time was somehow different, I had wanted to have an affair with someone. Even in that one afternoon, I had given a part of me to a stranger. Now I didn't care about having any feelings, it was just about having sex with someone else, what they could do for and to "me", and how they could make "me" feel. Simply put, NSA—no strings attached!

My selfishness needed to know what that was like. Now it was more about me having the power to dominate over a woman to rectify those feels of being dominated over by my mother. I wanted to feel like a master over a slave who must do as I say. No strings attached—just do what I want, make me feel empowered, get me off and I'll be done with you.

I'm not proud or happy about any of this. Even less as I relive my past thoughts and actions while I'm writing about them now. I would give anything to be able to go back and not make the same mistakes over and over again. However, if there is any good in all this, it must be found in the heart God has given me because of my life and my struggles.

Still, Lisa deserved none of the pain and hurt I've caused her. I know beyond a shadow of an doubt that I would give my life if it meant that all the pain and suffering would be gone forever in her life. That's the price that I would gladly pay for her total restoration.

Next is the third secret, perhaps my all-time rock bottom low, that I am not proud of, at all. Yet I must share if I'm going to be completely transparent. We all know what happens when you flirt with something long enough. There's an old saying, "If you play with fire long enough, sooner or later, you're going to get burned." I find it so ironic that it's been two years, on the very week, that I now write about what I consider my all-time rock bottom, low.

OUR STRUGGLES ARE REAL!

Our church had vacation bible school (VBS) in the evening time, which only makes sense as more parents are able to help out. Being no small event in a rather large church, people would bring food in for those helping. I'm sure there was nobody that left in the evenings hungry. Lisa had volunteered to help, plus our sons two girls were going to go to VBS. So it all worked out good, maybe too good.

Even with me working swing shifts, I could still go out to the church after work. I was working days on Tuesday and Wednesday that week, off on Thursday and Friday, and then back to nights on the weekend. That Wednesday, during my breaks at work, I saw an ad a woman had posted that intrigued my curiosity. I made contact as I shared my desires, and she shared her willingness to meet my demands. She would even be available around the time that I would be leaving work. All I had to do was give her a call, letting her know that I was going to come by.

Now I had been to this point before, even to the point that I was supposed to show up somewhere and I didn't. But that day, I knew Lisa was busy to the point she wouldn't be able to leave where she was at. For me to have to work over wasn't totally out of the norm. So when I got showered, changed, and out to my truck, I made the call. She was available and willing as she gave me her address.

Anxious, scared, excited, worried, the thrill, afraid—I experienced so many different emotions on my way to her place that evening. From the department store catalogs, playboy and penthouse magazines, phone sex lines, adult porn movies, XXX magazines, one night (day) stand, the thrill of the chase, seeing just how far I could get, to now actually having a sexual encounter with another woman. No strings attached, simply fulfilling as much carnal and lustful pleasure to make me feel superior. The woman was just the means to do whatever I commanded, to get me there and get me off.

Little by little, it never was quite enough. At each plateau, I found myself needing a little more to satisfy my quest for the ultimate sexual escapade. This time wasn't all that different, sure she made me feel like a god at that moment. Only thing was a few minutes later, as I left so did those feelings of empowerment—the "he" man feelings. None of it mattered on my way home. I felt dirty. Shame, guilt, self-condemnation and feeling unworthy swept over me as tears began to roll down my face. As a deep conviction invaded my heart, I knew that I could no longer continue down this same path anymore. Each step I took was digging a deeper hole.

Do you know what a deep, dark, empty hole is? It's a pit! Which is exactly where I was, walls of selfishness, digging through the mire of sex, alcohol, gambling, and anything else to make me feel good. If anyone wanted to get in my way, I had no problem pushing them away and putting them in their place.

It all had to stop, and stop *now*!

The momentary pleasures had never lived up to any of my expectations, they hadn't even come close! How stupid can anyone individual be? I had been taking the chance of losing the love of my life. So what if she didn't trust me? And that's only knowing what she knew. I knew for a fact that she shouldn't trust me. I wasn't sure if I should even trust myself. I was done, no more!

Once again, I turned to God, seeking His forgiveness. This time was going to be different! I knew that I couldn't handle anything on my own. This time, I completely surrendered my life, my will, my desires, my heart, everything. I placed all my hope, what little I had left, in God. I knew that things, the priorities in my life were going to have to change and God must be first, above all else. I'd been here before, but this time things were, NO, they had to be different. No more games!

Deep inside, I was actually allowing the Spirit of God to reside within me. I had a new and strong desire for His Spirit to burst forth in an undeniable way and to somehow use all the hurt and pain that I had caused for good. Was that even possible? I knew ultimately the war of good and evil had been won over two thousand years ago on a hill called Calvary. I earnestly wanted that victory in my life, understanding there would be battles. I began preparing, getting in the Word, spending time in prayer, and seeking His direction for my life.

I remembered, years ago, having an accountability partner. It hadn't worked back then with just the two of us, but what if it was a group of men, maybe it would work. I began to ask questions, making the suggestion of having a men's accountability group.

Maybe I wasn't asking the right people? I didn't understand. I had mentioned it to the men's ministry leader, so why did it appear to be no interest?

As for my home life, honestly, our marriage was struggling. Lisa's faith and trust in me had been completely destroyed long ago. That was with her only knowing part of my struggles, my secrets. She had no idea to what depths I had sunk to. My thought patterns and desires had become so twisted. I knew that the schedule I worked, days, nights, weekends, and twelve-thirteen-hour shifts weren't easy on our marriage. Plus, since my back issues, with the long days and preforming my job duties, I had my physical struggles, at least this time, they weren't sexual. Lisa and I began to pray about my job, about a way that we could be more active in our church. It was about that time when a straight day job opportunity came open.

If I was awarded the job, it would mean taking a substantial pay cut. However, the hours were Monday through Friday, 7:00 a.m. to 3:00 p.m. with the limited opportunity of overtime, off on the weekends, and home every night. It would make attending church so much easier. I could actually become active in church, which would help strengthen me spiritually. Not to mention that it would be easier on our marriage and family life.

As far as applying for the job, there was a process to go through, and I may not even get it. Lisa and I discussed it in length as the pay cut would certainly impact our lives. Our decision was for me to put in for the job, we would pray about it and may God's will be done. I never once did the math just to see how much of a pay cut it would be or how it would affect us. I was too afraid I would allow my mental reasoning to overrule my spiritual. No, I had to walk this one out in faith.

IronMen

Our church had three services on the weekend, one on Saturday evening and two on Sunday morning. The pastor had made a decision to start a fourth service on Sunday evening, which meant they were going to need someone to help with setting up and coordinating. I was all in and if I was to get the new position at work, it would work out. Awesome!

I would be working with the associate pastor as he was going to be in charge of the Sunday evening service. I was good with that. He was an all right guy, easy to talk with. In fact, we had several conversations that we just talked, nothing too deep or intellectual—still it was good to build trust and develop our relationship. In fact, it was in one of those conversations that I pitched the idea of the need to have a men's accountability group. I began to understand how beneficial it could be for men and to be completely honest and transparent, I needed it for myself! This time, I actually wanted accountability to work, I wanted to be held accountable.

We developed a plan; first—I would talk with the guy who had led a men's Bible study in the past, just to make sure that he had no plans of starting back up. I want to clear up one fact, a bible study and accountability/discipleship are two very separate things. Still, we didn't want anyone to feel like they were being pushed out. Second, I would put some feelers out to see if there were any other men interested in being a part of such a group.

The past leader was really too busy and didn't have the time. But he said that he would do anything that he could to help get a group started, admitting that it sounded like something that would be good for men.

I also discovered about a dozen guys that said they would be interested in a men's group. So I was excited to report back that everything was shaping up. We just needed a leader and the pastor's approval, and we'd be set!

As I shared my discoveries with the associate pastor, he commented that it sounded like we were all set. Wait a minute, we needed someone to lead the group, and don't we need to present this to the pastor? He probably needed to know what we were planning? To which the associate pastor replied, *Nope!*

That's one of the things that I came to love about that pastor, he didn't micromanage. The associate pastor went on to explain to me that when someone has an idea like this, the pastor was more than willing to let them "go with it." This wasn't at all what I had meant, remember I was going to blend in, not stand out. I realized the need to be in an accountability group, *not* lead one. I had opened my mouth, and now I was going to be the leader of this group. I wasn't sure about it, but I was willing to try. After all, that's all God needs—a willing heart.

We needed a name, some form of a mission statement, maybe even a scripture that would go along the lines of accountability. Several guys stepped up, and together this is what we came up with—IronMen.

> Iron sharpeneth iron; so a man sharpeneth the counte-

nance of his friend. (Proverbs 27:17, KJV)

Our mission statement was:

> To develop God-fearing, Bible reading men with fervent prayer lives. By creating strong brotherly bonds through sharing in one another's struggles and victories.

As men, it's hard for us to open up about our feelings and our personal battles—whether it be physical, mental, emotional, or spiritual. We grew up to be a *man*—macho, big and strong. Crying shows weakness, and to show weakness makes us vulnerable. It was phrases like, "If you want to cry, I will give you something to cry about!" and (as Dad cupped his hands) "Cry me a handful!" As a child there were times that I wanted to say something, I still remember being told, "Children are to be seen and not heard!" These words helped to harden me as I grew up. I dare say even teaching me an element of being secret.

Maybe we don't realize the damage that's done unintentionally. But somehow, it's there, subconsciously, and it affects our lives and every other life we come in contact with—specifically our wife, who God designed for us. Our children, who God has entrusted to us. Those around us who we are to love and respect. Yes the sin in our lives reflect negatively on how we treat others.

> The Lord God said, "It is not good for the man to be alone. I will make a helper suitable for him." (Genesis 2:18, NIV)

So God gave us (men), woman (our wife), to care for and to cherish.

> Husbands, in the same way be considerate as you live with your wives, and treat them with respect as the weaker partner and as heirs with you of the gracious gift of life, so that nothing will

> hinder your prayers. (1 Peter 3:7, NIV)

Not for a man to dominate over, but for her to be a help. And in a world *full of distractions* for us red-blooded American males, the struggles are real. Solomon the wisest man, perhaps ever, wrote:

> As iron sharpens iron, so one person sharpens another. (Proverbs 27:17, NIV)

It doesn't matter if you are sixteen, eighty, or somewhere in between. We *all* have struggles, and they are real. If we can talk openly and honestly sharing those struggles, we can learn from others, and we can draw strength from others' experiences. We can begin to understand we're *not* the *only* ones going through whatever issue you're dealing with. We can learn how others managed to walk through the same struggles that we ourselves encounter.

I can't emphasize enough how important it is to have trust in a group like this. It is *extremely important* that "what is said in the group, *stays* in the group."

> Therefore confess your sins to each other and pray for each other so that you may be healed. The prayer of a righteous person is powerful and effective. (James 5:16, NIV)

These are my goals/vision for IronMen:

1. We confess, sharing our weakness.
2. We pray for each other and our church body.
3. We build relationships with our brothers in Christ, based on trust and honor.
4. In doing this, we claim healing,—physically, mentally, emotionally, and spiritually.

We welcome the rewards of becoming better husbands, better fathers or grandfather, and a better, more Christ-like man! Maybe just maybe, if we as men *step up* and make a conscious decision to be more Christ-like, to fill the position God designed for men, we will begin to see:

1. Our prayers not being hindered.
2. Our nation healed.
3. Revival sweeping through our hearts, our families, our churches, our towns, and cities.

I would ask if anything that I have shared has struck a chord within you and your life?

- Are you the man that you desire to be?
- Is there room for improvement in your life??
- Are you as close to God as you desire to be?
- Do you want to be more like Christ?

Make the *commitment* to begin to become an IronMan.

OUR STRUGGLES ARE REAL!

This was one of the first IronMen descriptive posts that I shared to our church's Facebook page:

> There are rules for everything, what you might consider rules for the group is simple; Everything is scripture-based, No subject is off-limits and What's said in the group STAYS in the group. Trust is so very important in developing this type of group. For someone to share another's feelings and struggles could destroy lives and marriages. On more than one occasion I would emphasize the importance of "What's said in the group STAYS in the group."

During all this preparation to start this new group, I was awarded the straight day job that I had put in for. This cleared the way for me to lead the IronMen group and help with the Sunday evening service on a weekly basis. It truly was a new beginning for Lisa and I. We were more spiritually focused and Christ-centered. I didn't want to lead these guys astray, and I wanted to be sensitive to God's direction for the group. This led me to spend more time in prayer, seeking God's direction for each meeting, maybe it would have been easier to find a book, study guide, or devotional to go thru each week. That just didn't seem the direction that God wanted me to go. No, it had to come from the heart that God was giving me.

> I will give you a new heart
> and put a new spirit in you;
> I will remove from you your
> heart of stone and give you
> a heart of flesh. (Ezekiel
> 36:26, NIV)

Each week, God would place either a topic or scripture on my heart. I would allow that to develop in preparation for our next meeting. These topics and scriptures I later called a "springboard." We would open in prayer, do some small talk on what's going on in a general sense, and I would present the scripture or topic (springboard) opening it up for discussion. Often that would lead to someone opening up talking about something that was going on in their life.

I loved the fact we had a wide age range among the group. We're never too old or young to learn something. There may be someone that has gone through something that someone else is going through now. It wasn't that anyone was offering answers, only sharing life experiences and what or how they came threw through different situations. Maybe they would share a scripture that they have stood on.

It can be such a relief just to have someone to talk to, knowing that you won't be judged. Someone that will just listen and not feel they have to "fix you!" Someone that when you're ready, will offer Godly counsel. But for this to happen, you have to build trust in the group, that takes time. A true accountability group can be too large, six to no more than eight. It just makes the atmosphere more relaxed, easier for a guy to open up. For example, if you have five guys, meeting on a regular basis, they've established enough trust to begin to really open up. If you add a new guy to the mix, it can set the group back.

Who is this guy? Can we trust him? Will he sing like a canary to his wife when she asks how was the meeting? In some ways, you start all over in building trust. Granted this also depends on how open and honest the group of guys are. I want to caution you, as you don't want to turn anyone away just because they haven't been a part of the group before. It may be that they haven't heard anyone talking about others in the group so they feel it's a safe place. Be ever so sensitive to the Holy Spirit!

Our group started off fairly strong, but over the first six to eight weeks, our numbers dropped. Maybe they weren't ready to be open, perhaps it wasn't structured enough or they just didn't understand the direction we were going. It wasn't ever intended to be just another Bible study.

God gave me this scripture as an anchor and I continue to stand fast on it.

> Therefore confess your sins to each other and pray for each other so that you may be

healed. The prayer of a righteous person is powerful and effective. (James 5:16, NIV)

Accountability/ Discipleship

Do we really understand what it means to be accountable? The definition of accountability is the quality or state of being accountable especially an obligation or willingness to accept responsibility or to account for one's actions

John Wesley would always begin by asking, "How is it with your soul?" If people are truly open and honest with their answers, either then or now, the individual must first become transparent and vulnerable in opening up and share what truly is going on in their life. Everyone needs to be upfront with their struggles, trials, and even victories. It's just that it's easier said than done!

Transparency is a way of relating to another or in a group in which you reveal your inner self, your true experiences. That means exposing your vulnerabilities and fears, as well as your desires and point of view about whatever issues you're discussing or even facing. It also means that no one forces their point of view on anyone else. You can share, discuss and present your thoughts and convictions. But never attempt to force them on another as the solution.

> "Therefore, my dear friends, as you have always obeyed—not only in my presence, but now much more in my absence—continue to work out your salvation with fear and trembling," Philippians 2:12 NIV

The definition of vulnerable:

1. capable of being physically or emotionally wounded
2. open to attack or damage

Confessing our faults, struggles, and temptations to another person—this was

ACCOUNTABILITY/DISCIPLESHIP

what IronMen's about! I understood this as it's what God had laid on my heart. The group was open to discussions, and there were some that did share their struggles. It was only to a certain extent, it seemed that no one wanted to cross that invisible line, to go deeper.

I'll admit, I was open about having my sexual struggles. I just didn't go into the full details of how low I had sunken. In all of this, believing so strongly in accountability, I myself was unable to find *anyone* willing to step out and step up that I could go one on one with.

There was a person that knew a guy that was looking for a few men to surround himself with. I made the call to him, a total stranger with a mutual friend. I talked with him, on the phone that evening for over an hour. Finally a guy that got it and realized the importance of accountability. The only thing was, he wasn't local, it would have to be via phone or text, which I'm not a fan of. It's not that you can't hold someone accountable by a phone conversation or messaging, it's just easier for them to lie to you. It's being able to sit down with them and look them in their eyes, to be able to read their body language.

OUR STRUGGLES ARE REAL!

I'm not saying long-distance accountability won't work that way. I'm just saying it's not the ideal situation.

Between preparing for our group each week, communicating with this guy, and just feeling the responsibility to live out what I was "preaching" was enough to hold me accountable and true to the coarse. Sure, there were times that I had my battles, but God was changing my heart. For so many years, I had strangled my sensitivity, to become hard, not caring about or what others thought. I began to pray for a soft heart.

> His heart is as firm as a stone; yea, as hard as a piece of the nether millstone. (Job 41:24, KJV)

> I will give them a heart to know me, that I am the Lord. They will be my people, and I will be their God, for they will return to me with all their heart. (Jer. 24:7, NIV)

ACCOUNTABILITY/DISCIPLESHIP

Some of my hardest battles were with Lisa. Sure, she heard me say that I had changed. She saw me studying and in prayer more often. She also knew I'd been down this road before as a means to appease her. Was this just another temporary Band-Aid?

When I started my straight day position, I made a commitment to get up an hour earlier than I normally would and spend that time in devotion, reading my Bible, and prayer. Lisa saw all these things change in my life; unfortunately, as I said, I had been here before. She wanted to believe in me, but she just didn't trust me. And I do get it, but it's hard, I do want us to move forward. There are still times that I will do some little thing that mirrors a past action. I think it gives her "flashbacks" so I know it's hard on her as well.

I had destroyed a part of her, a part that I probably will never get back. However, we're still working on restoring our marriage, and I believe it will someday be better than ever before. It will never be the same as it was, but it will be better. Till then, I must remain focused, faithful, and assuring. It's the little thing that adds up, like not guarding my phone, not worrying about Lisa seeing what I'm looking at or who I'm messaging.

At one time, my phone wouldn't leave my possession. After all, I had things in it that Lisa didn't need to see, plus what if I got one of those off the wall messages. Now it's no big deal if I walk away and leave it laying. Besides, Lisa has my code to get into it anyway. Can you see the difference?

Even so, the depth of pain I've caused doesn't just go away overnight. Still, I struggle with that, I desire her approval, support, and trust. Oh, you think that's taking it too far? Let me pass along something a friend once shared with me. When you open your spiritual eyes and ears, it can penetrate the heart.

Helper in Greek or Hebrew translates to only four references:

1) God

> "So do not fear, for I am with you; do not be dismayed, for I am your God. I will strengthen you and help you; I will uphold you with

my righteous right hand." Isaiah 41:10 NIV

2) Jesus

"So we say with confidence, "The Lord is my helper; I will not be afraid. What can mere mortals do to me?"" Hebrews 13:6 NIV

3) Holy Spirit

"In the same way, the Spirit helps us in our weakness. We do not know what we ought to pray for, but the Spirit himself intercedes for us through wordless groans." Romans 8:26 NIV

4) Wife-help mate

"The Lord God said, "It is not good for the man to be alone. I will make a helper suitable for him."" Genesis 2:18 NIV

OUR STRUGGLES ARE REAL!

That's classifying your spouse in high ranking.

I wonder if I was to ask you where you would rank your spouse? Would you be honest to admit that she's further down the list than #4? Thing is, she can't be #1 either because then you have made her your idol. If this has made you think, perhaps it would be good to ask God to help you realign your priorities.

I continue to stay the course as I desire to grow spiritually. It is my heart's desire to know God personally and have His will in my life. Not only in my life but my family's lives, as well as the men in IronMen. We met at 7:00 p.m. at our church. I began to go in earlier just to have some alone time with God. We go through our day and so much can happen. I needed that time to adjust my thoughts, getting more focused on Him, the direction to go, to surrender the events of my day, good or bad over to Him. It was building a relationship with God.

People think it's hard to pray for an hour, it's so much more than just prayer. It's not just about asking God to meet your needs, other's needs, or giving Him thanks. Sometimes, we

ACCOUNTABILITY/DISCIPLESHIP

just need to shut up and listen! What's He trying to tell us? How else can we learn His voice? I came to enjoy that time alone with God.

Me, leaving early, triggered questions for Lisa—where was I going? Are you really doing what you say? How do I know you are where you say you are? All these questions were legitimate considering my past, still, her questions hurt.

IronMen had begun in November, and by April, attendance had leveled out to around five or six each week. While I struggled to understand the low attendance, how there seemed to be a lack of commitment, I did get it. "Life is busy."

I wanted each of the guys to know whether they could make the meetings or not. If they found themselves in a tight spot, struggling, facing those battles, men too often face and needed someone to talk with or just listen, I would be there. Not that I was anyone special, I've just been places that I don't want others to go.

The question came up if I planned to continue through the summer months. Too many times, when you put a hold on meetings, they never resume. I had come to love and appreciate each one of these guys—whether they were just members of our Facebook page or they had attended a meeting or regularly attended. I realized that May, June, and July were busy months while August and part of September may not be much better. However, I felt that it was important to continue, sure I would like to see each and every man attend. I knew attendance would vary as life keeps us busy, it keeps me busy.

My reasoning for continuing to meet through these months was simply they are some of the most trying for men and the struggles that we go through. Summer is hot, right? Women tend to wear fewer clothes, shorts, tube tops, swimwear, etc., all revealing body parts that when seen may trigger thoughts and desires. Yeah, the spring and summer months, in my opinion, is much more difficult on men.

It was around that same time God dropped it into my heart that we should have a men's conference. I had no idea how to put a conference together or who to get to speak, so again, I began to ask questions. I was trying to promote some interest and get some-

ACCOUNTABILITY/DISCIPLESHIP

one to take the lead. Most liked the idea and they even remembered that they had something similar several years ago. That's as far as it really went, no one had the time. The feeling that we needed to have a men's conference never really left me, in fact, the impression that we needed a men's event had only become stronger. Every chance I had, I would try to encourage different ones to get something started—after all, they had at least done this once before. There were several men in the church that liked the idea of having a men's conference. Still no one would step up and take the lead. What good is a good idea if it never gets any traction and dies?

I began to write out my life's testimony just to have an overview of where I've been—my pornography, sexual struggles, and how I believed that accountability was one of the key factors that had helped me. I was only highlighting the important issues, not going into any great depth of the details. At the time, writing out my testimony and trying to plan a men's conference was two completely separate events.

Once I had my story complete, I knew if I was to ever share my testimony in any detail at all, Lisa needed to be okay with it. Yes, I was a little nervous about what her response would be. Like a chicken, I forwarded it to her in a message. Evidently, as she read over it, she was questioning if I had posted this and if so who else had read it. Later, when we talked, I explained that for now, it was for her eye only. But at some point, I wanted to be able to share it with others; however, as our lives are intertwined, I wanted her to be okay with it first.

For about a month, it went back and forth. She would be okay with me sharing it to "No, you're not sharing it with anyone!" Finally, one day, she had a peace come over her about allowing me the freedom to share my story as so much of it involved her. It was written out in a rough draft form. No way was it ready to be presented in a message formation, but I had the general outline down.

In my spirit, I felt that having a men's conference would allow other men to understand words like "accountability," "transparency," and "vulnerability." It would bring them closer together, creating a stronger brotherly bond. Maybe they would understand why having a men's accountability group is ben-

ACCOUNTABILITY/DISCIPLESHIP

eficial to living a more godly life. It's not just about helping ourselves but helping others. We should be able to grasp the truth and the freedom found there, understanding the struggle is real.

> Then you will know the truth, and the truth will set you free. (John 8:32, NIV)
>
> This is the verdict: Light has come into the world, but people loved darkness instead of light because their deeds were evil.
> Everyone who does evil hates the light, and will not come into the light for fear that their deeds will be exposed.
> But whoever lives by the truth comes into the light, so that it may be seen plainly that what they have done has been done in the sight of God. (John 3:19–21, NIV)

What I did next was on impulse. I checked for an open date at the church, sometime in September. Having a church service on Saturday evenings ruled Saturday out, so let's go with a Friday evening,—not the best time, but when is? Friday, September 21, 2018, was an open date, so we penciled it in. I wasn't sure who we were going to have speak or who was going to do anything for that matter. I just knew God wanted us to have a men's conference, so we were going to have one. If I'm going to be the one putting it together, God had a lot of work to do.

Not Good Enough

In June, I was given the opportunity to preach on a Sunday evening. For the first time in almost twenty years. I had that longing to preach, I think it was in my spirit to do that which I had felt God once calling me to do. I just didn't see it happening—especially since it seems that most pastors are required to go to seminary. The door had opened to once again step up to the pulpit, at least one more time. I was honored to be allowed to preach the word of God in the manner of how I had perceived my calling years ago—a calling that I had never fully embraced, never quite stepping into.

God had been so good in reassuring me, it had been earlier in the year when our pastor had brought a message that hit me right between my eyes. He was talking about David, how he rejoiced when bringing the Ark of the

Covenant into Jerusalem, how Michal, his wife, Saul's daughter, had tried to shame him.

Can you believe our pastor? He even showed a movie clip of this scene. Now, remember what I shared about my experience, preaching years ago and the Bible college superintendent. It was as if God was reassuring me, literally telling me that I had been listening to Him. No matter what people may have thought or said that the message I had given some twenty years earlier, had been the right message that night.

I guess I had let the words people had spoken affect my life and confidence more than I even realized or cared enough to admit. All we can do is follow His direction, making sure it lines up with scripture. After all those years, God cared enough about me to give me confirmation.

I found out about a men's conference going on locally. The only thing was I found out the day it was happening, still, I had to try to check it out. One of the guest speakers was Voddie Baucham. I had heard some of his teachings and I thought how awesome it would be to hear him speak in person. All of his teachings that I had heard were "kick your butt" good at least they did mine. They weren't always comfortable words but they were anointed by God and always spoke to me. It was late enough in the conference that I was able to slip in, (at no charge), sure enough, he was speaking.

You may recall me saying how sometimes I'll capture a thought, something that is so good that it sticks with me. I've used this saying multiple times since hearing Reverend Baucham say it that day. "We all need to be disciples, discipling, disciples!" Young or old, maybe twenty years ago, you could have used someone to disciple you, what are you doing now? Are we being a hypocrite? I know I've paraphrased this, but it made an impact. I knew no matter how discouraging it was to see the guys' lack of interest in IronMen and accountability, God was shaping and softening my heart to reach out and disciple men. The very thing that could have helped me, twenty years earlier, had I only realized and accepted it

I didn't know where to start, to put a men's conference together, plus, we were operating with little to no funds. It was going to cost money to get someone to come speak unless I spoke. I really wasn't sure about sharing my heart, my struggles on stage, before a large group of men. Sure I had preached before, somehow I thought this was different.

Fortunately, I had a friend that was good with computers and was willing to help out. As we began to make up some flyers, we realized that we needed a title or topic for the conference. I wanted it to appeal and be relatable to men—"The struggle is real!" It had a ring to it and just maybe it would catch guys' attention, stirring up their curiosity.

The other thing was, I didn't want people to feel like it was a denominational conference. It wasn't a Method, Baptist, Assembly, Nazarene, Full Gospel, Pentecostal, nondenominational, or any other church thing—it was about the body of Christ, His Church. I didn't care where they went to church, for that matter, I didn't even care if they even went to church. I want them to understand that every man struggles with something, and we need to be willing to help others and allow others to help us.

It was becoming apparent that I was to be the speaker for the conference. This was the very heartbeat God had given me because of my past. Every one of us has a story, and our story has shaped who we are. It has given us the heart to reach others that are in situations that we used to be in. Our story has made us relatable, and we should have compassion and a greater understanding of those that are where we ourselves were at one time.

I hadn't shared my story at least openly and in detail before a large group. Understand that I had no problem sharing in a one on one situation, but this was going to be an entirely different level.

One thing that I found to be so refreshing and awesome in our IronMen group. Was that while there were some guys that, in my opinion, just didn't get it. There was especially one guy that I felt a connection with; however, due to his job, he had to travel a lot. What I found to be an incredible example of dedication was, he could just be getting home from being gone three or four days. His first stop even before going home would be to come to our meeting. It was the little things like that which was a huge encouragement to me.

Back to the conference preparations—I knew a guy, well that's a stretch, actually, we had grown up in the same town. He had been on a praise and worship team in church and he also had a band that played together. I reached out and explained what we were doing, asking him if they would consider playing four or five songs. When they finally committed, we had everything set, the plan was to feed their bodies, worship God, let them know that their not alone in their struggles and challenge them to examine their life. I would be leading by example from my own life experiences, reinforcing live changing points with scriptures.

Let me back up for just a moment—those four months leading up to the conference were busy. Just in my preparation to speak was enough to keep me busy in my spare time. Sure, I knew my story, however, I felt like I needed to form an outline. I wanted to be sure that it would flow, after all, I wanted the conference to be top-notch, to say the least.

> For from him and through him and for him are all things. To him be the glory forever! Amen. (Romans 11:36, NIV)

I wrestled with God about me speaking right up to the day of the conference. I didn't feel worthy, who was I? I had been to men's conferences before—the big names, professional football players, and big-time coaches sharing their stories. I must admit it was pretty cool, but just one thing—I didn't relate to those guys! I'm just a common every day Joe, working a dead-end job to support my family the best I can. I'm sorry but as awesome as some of those guys' stories may have been, I just didn't connect with them. You have to be relatable if you expect to connect with people!

As I wrestled with the thought of me leading this conference, not feeling good enough or educated enough. God dropped this question in my heart, "Who did I call to be my disciples? Fishermen, common everyday guys, most were uneducated but "ALL" were willing!" That's right, just common every day guys, just like me. It was at that point I got it, and I was willing!

I went to our pastor, sharing the itinerary I had planned for the evening. After all, it was being held in his church, and he wanted it to flow smoothly as well. I believe he was a little surprised at how well we already had things laid out. His one piece of advice was to not hold it too long. From his experience, if you speak over twenty minutes, you begin to lose people.

While I agreed and went on, my mind was racing. There was no way possible that I could share my life in 20 minutes, not effectively. What was I going to do?

I hadn't really thought about the actual time, sure I had allowed an hour, but I had never spoken for that long. Maybe I would be able to speak for forty to forty-five minutes and give people time to ask questions or just be running ahead of schedule. Now he was expecting me to hold my time down.

Going Live

Within this same three-month period, I had shared my story with three different men. One understood as he shared my desire to see pornography and sexual-based sins addressed within the church. He himself had actually helped host several men's conferences and was a great help and inspiration to me. He gladly gave me some tips and pointers and helped in spreading the word about the IronMen conference. I remember asking him how many of the flyers, announcing the conference he was going to want. I almost fell over when he said fifty.

I made it a point to get any advice that I could from him. As we met for coffee one evening, I shared my concern about trying to hold my time down to only twenty minutes. His response only confirmed the feelings I had in my spirit. "It's sometimes easier to ask for forgiveness than it is permission. You must allow His Holy Spirit freedom to move, just share what God has laid on your heart. Don't worry about the length or time, it will be alright." This man was such an encouragement for me during this time.

The second person that I encountered, was a younger guy. While we were simply talking, my spirit picked up on something this guy said. I began to open up about my struggles with pornography. That's when I saw in his eyes as they lit up. "You mean other guys struggle with this too?" Satan had isolated him in guilt and shame, reinforced by condemnation that a pastor of a church had laid on him.

That's right, Satan will use any means possible to achieve his agenda, even a "Christian." I made time to meet with him, one on one. I was real about my past struggles. I didn't pull any punches as I shared the ugly truth of my journey and the pain I had put my wife through.

It was like I was looking into a mirror of myself some twenty years earlier. Then when I met his wife, I recognized that look on her face. I had seen that same look in my

Lisa's eyes. I could see the pain, hurt, and disappointment that filled her eyes. My heart ached not only for them but for my own wife. That's what I had put her through and it wasn't very pretty.

Sad thing was, his response was the same that mine was years earlier. He had shared his struggles and heard about mine. He may not have verbally said it, but I could read his body language. He figured that he was good now. All I could do was pray and let him know that I was there if he ever needed to talk.

In this third account, God actually directed me to someone. Lisa and I had got away and gone to a four-day church conference. It was after the first service that I felt the gentle nudging of the Holy Spirit directing me to talk with and pray for this man, a total stranger. As I wrestled with the thought, I couldn't do that, I had never even met the man. Over the next couple of days, our paths continued to cross several times. Even though we never actually spoke every time I turned around, there he was. Still, I just wasn't sure, what if I was wrong? I pleaded with God for a sure sign that I should approach this guy.

Almost as if God hadn't made it plain enough already.

It was the final night of the conference. One more opportunity was given as he and his wife sat down two rows in front of Lisa and I. How much clearer did it need to be? I knew what I had to do, I couldn't wait for that message to be over. As the service closed there were many people that went to the front for prayer, I went to talk with this man, a total stranger.

As I approached him, I apologized for not coming to him earlier as I had been too busy wrestling with God. He understood, but he was all right now, he had a migraine headache and someone else had prayed with him. I stood there, looking at him, slowly shaking my head no. "No, that's not it, there's more." As I just stood there, looking at him in his eyes.

Then he broke, sharing how he was a pastor, and he was struggling with pornography. He didn't have anyone that he could share this with. If he was to share this with the wrong person, it would jeopardize his position and his livelihood. He really wanted to break free, and he even understood how having someone to hold him accountable could be helpful. He explained how he and a couple of other pastors had gotten together and shared, up to a point. None of them had been willing to cross that line of complete transparency. There just wasn't anyone that he felt comfortable enough with to share all of this. He really wasn't even sure why he was sharing this with me.

I explained my story in short to him. I told him the heart that God had given me, how, as we expose and shed light on our addictions, all that guilt, shame, and condemnation lose its grip. How that I believed in accountability and how I had found freedom in shedding light and exposing my struggles, I understood how he felt. If there was no other reason for being where I was at that moment, it was for him. It was a divine appointment set by God.

We shared, we prayed, and we exchanged contact information, granted long-distance accountability isn't ideal. It's way too easy to not tell everything, where if you're face-to-face, you can read people, and in your spirit, you can tell. I'm not even sure that he really even expected me to follow up with him.

But for the next six months, we regularly messaged. While it wasn't quite to the depth, I would have liked, if it was helping him. That's all that really mattered! There were times that he confessed stumbling when he could have kept silent. It was in those times that I knew he was serious.

Then one day, I received that message, he had found someone there where he lived that he could sit down with and be open, honest, and transparent with. As excited that I was for him, this was an answer to our prayers, I admit that I was also a little skeptical. I didn't want him to get hurt. As a pastor, he had so much at stake. Could this guy be trusted? I knew ultimately it was his decision if he felt good about it, then okay. I still wanted to stay in contact with him. It was important for me to know that he knew that I would always be there for him.

From time to time, when God lays it on my heart, I'll still send him a message. He will probably always remain in my prayers, and I will always consider him a friend, that's how deep our brotherly bond is. Really, as Christians, isn't that the way it should be?

After I had written about this third encounter, I felt impressed to reach out to my friend. I explained how God had laid it on my heart to write my life's story of my addictions and struggles.

I've been purposely vague in situations not to expose anyone's identity while being completely accurate in giving an account of the struggles. Remember, in accountability, it's not about being secretive, it's about being confident that no one else is going to share my story. It's building that trust, knowing what I share stays with that person or persons, depending on if it's a group situation.

I had originally left out the part about him being a pastor even though that can be so impactful in giving others hope. The statics don't lie, 58% of pastors themselves struggle with pornography.

I shared what I had written about our journey together, asking for his permission to share even as vague as I had made it. There was no way that I was going to break his trust. The following is his words:

> Hi, Rick. You have my permission and you can add that

> it was a pastor you talked with. That he was suppose to be leading his people in righteousness and holiness but most weeks he stood in the pulpit with hidden shame. Now that he has been set free, people in the congregation are asking why his sermons seem so different, so powerful, so anointed. Also, he has found a new joy and enthusiasm for the Word of God and for sermon preparation. He has a new confidence that God is Leading him again. Any man, pastor or church member, who thinks God can use them while living in sin is lying to themselves. The joy of being set free and being used by God again is greater than the shame of admitting your sin.

That in itself was such a blessing, for God to use me in such a powerful way. It only proves His power when we are willing to surrender our lives over to Him.

One Sunday morning before church I had yet another guy ask, just what is IronMen? As I went through my explanation, I explained the importance of accountability and how we must be honest and become transparent in all that we do. How even John Wesley would begin a meeting by asking, a lot of times, "How is it with your soul?" In fact, Wesley had five specific questions that he would ask, which sounds a lot like accountability to me.

This guy that I was talking with made the comment that it sounded a lot like AA. I hadn't viewed it as an addiction before, but it did make sense. I was beginning to see a clearer picture of my sin that I had struggled with for so very long. The grip that it had on my life, yes it was an addiction.

The other part of the preparation for the IronMen conference was music. Yes, we had a band; however, I thought that it would be a good idea to have something playing in the background as everyone was arriving. One day, Lisa told me that she heard a song that would be good for the conference. As I listened to this song, I must have played it over at least five times. It would be perfect for a theme song for IronMen.

Over the next couple of months, as a song would catch her attention, she would write down the title and that night she would want my opinion. After all, she was the one person that knew exactly what the conference was about. We reached a total of nine songs that could speak to the very soul of a man. Just FYI, I only choose one of those songs. Lisa had tuned in and captured what I considered the heartbeat of the conference. In a sense, playing those songs could set the entire tone for the night.

We had all the bases covered from our cook and kitchen help, sound and audio guys, parking lot and greeters, security, and a master of ceremonies. We were as ready as we ever would be.

The night before the conference, the band set up and did their final practice. I had given them a general rundown about the conference topic, only encouraging them to just let the spirit lead in choosing what songs to play. Oh my! As I listened to the words of those songs, every one of them fit with the message. It was amazing no it was definitely God. As for the band themselves, they rocked!

I had taken the day of the conference off. I knew there was still a lot to make sure was done by 6:00 p.m. Lisa and one of the guys did the grocery shopping. Later that morning, the cook came in and began the prep work. We got the seating and tables to eat at set-up. We were going by faith because I had never done an event like this. We had absolutely no idea how many guys to expect.

We had pushed announcing the conference; however, we didn't have any kind of preregistration. (I would highly recommend having preregistration), I had estimated that if only half the men in the church alone showed up that would be around 100 plus men. And we had reached out beyond our own four walls, hoping to reach around 150 men. We knew it could be more or less. Despite feeling that every man could benefit by attending, our prayer was for every man that had heard about the conference that needed to be there, would be there.

I had my one new friend who had been a help and encouragement along this journey. He had offered so many encouraging words of wisdom that had helped. I had also reached out to the man that twenty years earlier was willing to be a support for me. I extended a personal invitation, even though that was so long ago, he had played a part in all this. Both these men were there that night, along with another guy that I had been holding accountable.

We didn't have the numbers I had hoped for. There were only around sixty-five men in attendance with less than half those who attended church there. Keep in mind, this church has 1400 members on the registry. Now you can understand my disappointment. Still, I believed in the message and that God had a purpose for us having this conference.

> And we know that in all things God works for the good of those who love him, who have been called according to his purpose. (Romans 8:28, NIV)

Everything flowed well, sure, we had a couple of hiccups, nothing noticeable. Everyone enjoyed the band as they lead us into His courts with praise. While my mind raced, there was a calm in my spirit and I could sense the Spirit of God there.

I had my outline, but I was still allowing the Holy Spirit to lead. There were things that I had written down that I didn't share, and there were things that I shared that I didn't have written down.

I had considered what my pastor had shared about holding my message to twenty minutes. In my outline, I had broken it up into three sections. The first part laid the groundwork, which was about fifteen minutes. To break it up, I had what I called our theme song played, which lead to the testimony of my life's struggles. When I came to the third part, I took a moment to ask God if I should close or continue. I had no idea how long I had been speaking, it really didn't seem that long. I felt the Spirit leading me to proceed with my message, showing that we can find accountability, even in the Old Testament.

As I wrapped up my message, I had hopes of men desperately desiring to obtain the freedom that I had found. I felt it important to give an invitation, an opportunity for all

OUR STRUGGLES ARE REAL!

to find freedom in whatever they were struggling with. Not one man came forward that night. I could only take comfort in knowing that I had completed what God had placed on my heart. I knew seeds had been sown.

A Warrior Stands

There were a lot of positive comments, which was assuring. It just saddened me knowing there were guys there that had passed up an opportunity to find a freedom that night. No, I'm not passing judgment. It's just that when you hear that a teenage boy made the comment, "I think he's talking about me!" Then to hear the adults' answer, and I'm not even sure the adult realized what he was confessing. As he answered, "I think he's talking about all of us!"

As I heard that, my Spirit quickened to the fact that both these guys were struggling.

In my one friend's opinion, from his experience of conferences, this one was a success. Seeds had been planted, and there was a lot for the men to consider, but only time would tell. I did after all feel at peace about the conference, how everything had gone and what I had shared.

It was a few days later when I found out that I had spoken for sixty minutes. You know, never once did my pastor make a comment one way (good) or the other (bad) about any part of the conference. Yes, while I had shared my story, the focus was God and what He had brought me out of. Still, it would have been nice if the pastor had given me some kind of feedback. Even to this day, I'm not sure exactly what he thought.

What I do know is some people began to treat Lisa and me differently. It felt as though we had gone from being close to people to some of those same people that were now holding us at arm's length away. I didn't notice it as much as Lisa did, maybe it's because she's more of a people pleaser or just more in tune with some things. I don't mean that in a bad way, but she's just more sensitive like that.

A couple of months before the conference, I had reached out to a pastor friend. He was the one that had been our pastor back when I had gone to Bible college. Thing was, he had reached out to us when I was down with my back the second time around. They were starting a new church and was wondering if we would be interested in being a part of a new church. Timing can mean everything, if it had been a couple of months earlier, maybe. But by that time, we had locked in where we were attending. It just didn't feel right to up and change churches. Besides at that time, I was still dealing with, and struggling in my addictions.

We meet up for breakfast on a Saturday morning. Where we caught up on how life, church, and our families were doing. I told him what was going on in our life and invited him and any of the men at his church to come to the IronMen conference. He said that he wouldn't be able to make the conference due to a scheduling conflict, but he would pass it along.

When our schedules would allow, we would get together for breakfast from time to time. Saturday mornings was the only time we could meet up, and that was spotty. But it was always good just to visit and catch up. I always appreciated the fact he was willing to give up some of his time to get together.

One week, we had made plans to meet for breakfast; however later he messaged me.

He had forgotten that their men's group was meeting that Saturday. So he invited me to come check out their group if I wanted. Sure, why not? I didn't have any problem visiting another church's men's group. Besides I could actually sit back and enjoy being a participant instead of a leader. This was another opportunity to soaking in more of God. Their group was more like a devotional study, but different as they used more videos. Of course, their topic of discussion was geared towards men. It was a good change of pace. I even felt like I fit in.

I floated along for the next month, encouraged by what God had allowed me the privilege of being a part of. Curious about what might be next, it would be so much easier if God would just give us a roadmap for our life.

> Your word is a lamp for my feet, a light on my path. (Ps. 119:105, NIV)

We can only see the path that is before us—not very far down the road at all. That's where our faith comes in, if we knew what was ahead, good or bad, what would we change? Because it's only natural to try to compensate in an attempt to either avoid something or make something happen.

I had the opportunity to go to a men's retreat about a month after our conference. It was about the right size for an accountability group. Although it was supposed to help break down barriers, there were two of us that had no problems sharing our struggles.

I remember on multiple occasions my wife, Lisa, asking why would I do the things I had done. Was she not attractive enough? What had she done? Was I not happy? And at first, I really didn't have an answer, but later, I decided that I had just been stupid and selfish. Going to that weekend gave me a much better understanding of "why" I had done some of the things I had done. Example— how, when you view pornography, there are certain electrodes in the brain that will weld together, taking about seven days for those to begin to release. If you view more pornography, they will again wield together, forming a stronger bond.

Another point is if you do an MRI of a brain on alcohol, drugs, or pornography, they all look the same. If you consider these two points, in my mind, there is no question—it really is an addiction.

While the weekend supplied a lot of good information, it was also scripture-based. There was time to reflect, learn about yourself and drawing closer to God. For me, it was one of the most spiritual weekends that I have had. I understood my sonship with God as my Father, in a much deeper and more personal way. I had such an overwhelming peace in my heart and soul.

Here are my notes from what I heard God speaking to me:

> Some encouraging words that I received from God this weekend!
>
> In praying for wisdom and understanding, that it's not to be as a tool or weapon, but as a guard and guide.
>
> Being a lover, not a fighter bypasses learning to be a warrior.

A WARRIOR STANDS

To be a lover is easier, more pleasurable.

To be a warrior requires effort like training for a sport.

In never learning the value of the strengths of a warrior or recognizing your weakness, you didn't learn the value of taking a stand. To have the support of your brother. Warriors stand his, no, they stand their ground. There is no other option, either stand or die trying!

Just as the Roman soldier, their armor was made to stand, to join together and press forward.

That is why you continue to circle, returning to the same spot, never fully learning those lessons needed to complete the tasks and battles that lay ahead.

Learn to embrace, to love.

Care and compassion.

Then you can move on. Your building on your life's story. That foundation is now strong.

The wind blows as my spirit does. Gentle and refreshing. Directing our paths, sometimes that direction changes, but my spirit is always there. Even in times of storms, my wind, my spirit, helps move those storms through our life.

You can't have the storm without my wind. But you can always have my spirit, storm or no storm.

I really hated for that weekend to be over! It was back to life as normal, no conferences to prepare for or retreats to look forward to. I was on a spiritual high after that retreat weekend. I had found a mountaintop with God and I wanted to stay there. The thing about it is, while it' s refreshing and the view is spectacular on the mountain, growth comes from the valleys.

Even though I walk through the darkest valley, I will fear no evil, for you are with me; your rod and your staff, they comfort me. (Ps. 23:4, NIV)

The Attack

I had gotten back from the retreat on Sunday afternoon. It was now Thursday evening at our weekly IronMen group meeting. I was still riding that spiritual high from my weekend. My prayer time prior to the group was so relational with Dad. Let me explain that. Jesus taught the disciples to pray, saying, "Our Father," probably because that's the way they talked back then.

I personally never went to my dad and said, "Father, I need this or that." My father was Dad to me, for others, it may be daddy, pops, or a number of different names, which all refer to father. So if knowing God as our Father is going to be about our relationship, why shouldn't we make it personal and intimate? Some may claim that using the term, "Father," shows a certain amount of respect. I won't disagree with that, there are times to address God as Father. However, when referring to God as Dad for myself makes it more personal.

Back to the group that night. We had our normal meeting with prayer, our springboard scripture, and discussion. Somewhere out of the clear blue one of the guys ask my thoughts on suicide.

Really, that's a loaded question, as I shared "my" belief on the subject. Explaining that in *my opinion*, if someone is of sound mind, suicide is undoubtedly a sin. We are made in the image of God.

> So God created mankind in his own image, in the image of God he created them; male and female he created them. (Gen. 1:27, NIV)

By taking your own life, you are no more than destroying the very image of God.

> If anyone destroys God's temple, God will destroy that person; for God's temple is sacred, and you

together are that temple.
(1 Cor. 3:17, NIV)

You shall not murder.
(Exod. 20:13, NIV)

I firmly believe that it is murdering yourself, therefore you are guilty of killing. Thou shall not kill! So in my personal interpretation, It's a sin with a one-way ticket to hell.

From that point on, it became a downward spiral. He informed me that he had already talked with the pastor and one of the associate pastors about this. According to him, they agreed with him that suicide was permissible. Again, I stated that "in my opinion, it was wrong!" It later hit me, if he had already talked with the pastor, why even ask me? I really felt as if I'd been set up.

Then he mentioned "self-gratification" and how it's not a sin. Perhaps, my attitude was wrong by that point, but he heard my story six weeks earlier. I remembered all my struggles with masturbation, self-gratification, or (let's just be open and honest) "jacking off,"—it doesn't matter what you call it. It's all the same thing, sin is sin. All the guilt

THE ATTACK

and shame it had brought in my life. I wasn't coming off the fact it's a sin and that makes it wrong to do.

Seriously think about what he had called it,—"self-gratification." If you let your "self" get in the way of anything, it's going to become sin.

Selfishness:

> Idolatry and witchcraft; hatred, discord, jealousy, fits of rage, selfish ambition, dissensions, factions. (Gal. 5:20, NIV)

> For where you have envy and selfish ambition, there you find disorder and every evil practice. (James 3:16, NIV)

Gratifying:

> So I say, walk by the Spirit, and you will not gratify the desires of the flesh. (Gal. 5:16, NIV)

> Rather, clothe yourselves with the Lord Jesus Christ, and do not think about how to gratify the desires of the flesh. (Rom. 13:14, NIV)

Sexual Immorality:

> Flee from sexual immorality. All other sins a person commits are outside the body, but whoever sins sexually, sins against their own body. (1 Cor. 6:18, NIV)

> It is God's will that you should be sanctified: that you should avoid sexual immorality. (1 Thess. 4:3, NIV)

> For it is from within, out of a person's heart, that evil thoughts come—sexual immorality, theft, murder. (Mark 7:21, NIV)

THE ATTACK

> Put to death, therefore, whatever belongs to your earthly nature: sexual immorality, impurity, lust, evil desires and greed, which is idolatry. (Col. 3:5, NIV)

This is how I would describe sexual immorality—the evil ascribed to sexual acts that violate social conventions, intentionally going against accepted ideas of what is right. If these scriptures weren't enough, these next ones should remove any doubt.

Debauchery is an extreme indulgence in bodily pleasures and especially sexual pleasures.

Excessively indulgent in sensual pleasures.

> The acts of the flesh are obvious: sexual immorality, impurity and debauchery. (Gal. 5:19, NIV)

> I am afraid that when I come again my God will humble me before you, and I will be grieved over many who have

> sinned earlier and have not repented of the impurity, sexual sin and debauchery in which they have indulged. (2 Cor. 12:21, NIV)

Debauchery is a noun, meaning crazy partying and wild nights, usually accompanied by a lot of alcohol. Debauchery is all about indulging in some of life's pleasures—overindulging, in fact.

> Do not get drunk on wine, which leads to debauchery. Instead, be filled with the Spirit. (Eph. 5:18, NIV)

> Let us behave decently, as in the daytime, not in carousing and drunkenness, not in sexual immorality and debauchery, not in dissension and jealousy. (Rom. 13:13, NIV)

> For you have spent enough time in the past doing what

> pagans choose to do—living in debauchery, lust, drunkenness, orgies, carousing and detestable idolatry. (1 Peter 4:3, NIV)

His words cut me to the heart as he told me multiple times how I was lacking in knowledge. How really if I was going to be any kind of leader, teacher or minister at all, that I needed to go to seminary.

Then finally I realized that I was arguing with a religious spirit. On one hand, I felt bad because I had let him push all the right buttons to get me stirred up. Still, I knew what I believed. I had stated that the suicide issue was "my opinion." I did not waiver from my beliefs or my convictions. Eventually I realized we were getting nowhere fast. In an attempt to deescalate the situation, I simply suggested that we should just agree to disagree on these matters and dismissed the group.

As we left that night, there were a few of us still discussing the suicide issue as we walked out. We were in agreement that while it was a touchy subject, we really wouldn't want to take that gamble, not with eternal life hanging in the balance.

As I drove home, I continued to be both disappointed in how I had handled the entire situation and glad that I had stood my ground based on my convictions. I hadn't even been home ten minutes when I received a message from him. He had found a clip on YouTube from someone that claimed to be a part of the denomination of the church we were attending at the time, who supported his view on suicide.

Why was it so important for me to change my convictions to agree with him? Show me scriptures that supports your case, and I'll agree. I know I don't understand a lot of modern technology; however, I am smart enough to know if you search hard enough, you can find someone to agree with anything. I also realize when you come under conviction, you yourself can choose to live in denial. I should know, I had lived there for years. Then again, if you can prove, at least in your mind, someone is wrong in one point, it becomes easy to discredit anything and everything they say and believe.

THE ATTACK

To this day, I believe that the issue wasn't so much suicide, it was the same struggle that I had battled with myself for years. That same battle carries on worldwide today among men and women. We justify our actions because the Bible doesn't word it the way that we label it in today's words.

That's why our relationship with God is so very important. There are people that read and know the Bible, but if you don't have a relationship with God, when you don't allow His Spirit to lead, guide, and direct your understanding, allowing the Holy Scriptures to come alive.

His word *never* changes—it's our understanding that changes as we grow. I believe that if the moment we accepted Jesus as our Lord and Savior, He poured out complete revelation and holiness, we would be so overwhelmed our minds would literally overload. Our pursuit of God and His Holiness is progressive, step-by-step, as we grow spiritually becoming more Christ-like.

I know I'm not the same person/Christian that I was three years ago. Just as I hope I'm not the same person/Christian I am now in three more years. Understand that I used the term "three years" as a figure of speech. My desire and I pray that it's you're desire too, is to grow closer and more Christ like each day.

To "just" read the Bible is an act of religion and being religious. That entire situation was overwhelming despite the fact that I knew who I was in Christ. It didn't matter that I had personally already worked through my own doubts and feelings of not being educated enough. My world, my faith and my identity had been questioned. I felt disrespected by one man before everyone that was there that night.

It had rocked my world, but I didn't back down. If you don't stand for something, you will fall for anything! I had based my opinions and my beliefs on scripture. Strangely enough, he didn't want to take this to the pastor. He also didn't feel he had disrespected me in any way, and he was only trying to "help" me.

His solution was to stop coming since I was lacking in knowledge, not willing to be open-minded. Maybe I shouldn't have reacted in the manner that I did. Perhaps, I shouldn't have let the whole thing slide and went to our pastor.

THE ATTACK

I had always expressed how whatever is shared in the group stays in the group. Now that was being tested, if I was to go to the pastor, what kind of message would that send? I felt that he had been looking for an excuse to stop coming, and I let that happen.

For the next month, I really struggled in my prayer life. I continued to go early before IronMen to spend time with God, but it was really hard. I just kept on pressing, and there were times I didn't have the words. I just knew that I was not going to give up.

> Therefore, there is now no condemnation for those who are in Christ Jesus, (Romans 8:1, NIV)

I continued to attend my pastor friend church's men's group on the first and third Saturdays. It was helping me in getting my focus back, knowing who I was, who I am in Christ. No matter how hard I tried, I just couldn't go in, sit down, listen, and then leave. Thankfully, they seemed to appreciate my input as my comments, opinions, and views appeared to be welcome.

OUR STRUGGLES ARE REAL!

I became increasingly more comfortable with this new group, as my interest sparked. They had several quotation signs, We're all about the "capital C" church! We will be known for what we are for, not what we are against, and To lead people to become fully devoted followers of Christ. This is three out of about seven such signs. All of them had a strong sense of commitment to God for the purpose of reaching people.

Lisa was content and active in our church. She was helping cook for a weekly dinner, filling in and cleaning the church from time to time. Lisa had made a lot of friends, impacted lives, she has always been able to connect well with seniors. She is most definitely a lady with many talents. Still. there had been a shift after the conference that even she recognized.

While some held me at a distance, my heart continued to soften. I knew now more than ever how men are bound by guilt and shame and how the church is slowly being destroyed from within, and most don't even realize it. I didn't want to be like:

> I looked for someone among them who would build up

> the wall and stand before me in the gap on behalf of the land so I would not have to destroy it, but I found no one. (Ezek. 22:30, NIV)

If there's no one else, then I must step up. I must be accountable, transparent even becoming vulnerable, no more secrets. Please, Lord, find me worthy to "stand in the gap."

I was hungry for more of God, desiring for Him to use me. I became comfortable with this new bunch of guys. It seemed that they too wanted more of God. It wasn't long before Lisa and I began attending their early Sunday morning service. We would leave there and attend our churches late service, double-dipping in God. On more than one occasion, the two messages would parallel each other, *awesome*. There were things in both churches we loved, just as there were things that we questioned in both.

As time passed, there was small talk about their church growth. One day, after the men's group, I was told that there was a place there for us to serve if we should ever choose. Even the men's group leader had given me the impression that I would be more than welcome to help co-lead the group. I had shared my heart, my struggles, and how men can find freedom if they chose. How God had given me the heart to help other men like myself, finding freedom from a place that I once had been.

On more than one occasion, their group leader and I had stayed after the meeting and talked, one on one. I was always open, honest, and transparent with him, making myself vulnerable and accountable. How can I not be any of these things if I'm going to ask others to be that way?

All these little comments, possible opportunities, were they open doors? Was this God, lighting my path?

There was still the hurt from the guy from our IronMen group. As I questioned myself, was I in some way wanting to run from that? I was aware that people treated us differently after the conference. As much as I loved our pastor, and I still love him, I could be sharing something via text or messenger. He would engage in general and faith-based conversation, but let me share about an article or mention anything about pornography and sexual types of sin, "crickets," nothing.

As I began to seek God's will and direction for our lives, I earnestly prayed. Not just including it in my prayers but spending time in prayer about where God would have us serve. Lisa had found her place of service, a purpose, and she was content in going where we were at. Or was I just being selfish?

To be honest and transparent, I had been in a place like this before, but somehow, it was different this time. Before, I had simply gotten my eyes off Jesus and on people. Before, when I had been hurt by people and their words, I had taken it personally. Before, when people stood in judgment of me, I simply hated them back, allowing anger and bitterness to overcome and consume me. But not this time!

I prayed hard about making a change in churches, and I counted the cost. I would be walking away from the IronMen group. Granted, it never fully developed into the accountability group that I had intended. It was more along the lines of a Bible study but still, it could impact lives. I had a guy that could step up as the leader and carrying on with IronMen.

Perhaps the greatest cost wasn't even mine, it would be Lisa. She would be giving up multiple opportunities that brought her joy, a sense of self-worth, and accomplishment.

I wasn't taking this decision lightly, I needed to be sure that I was hearing the voice of God—that it was His Holy Spirit leading me, *not* me falling back into who I use to be, reacting in anger, out of spite.

It was after praying and praying some more that I surrendered. I came to a place that I just didn't worry about it. Later came the peace that we should change churches—the opportunity to serve others and help lead men, all the things that God has laid on my heart.

I knew in my spirit what we needed to do. I was willing to compromise, and we could attend one church on Saturday evenings and the other on Sundays. This would allow us to keep a foothold in both churches. It wasn't like being in sin and trying to keep one foot in the church and the other one in the world. I made this suggestion to Lisa for her thoughts.

It was one or the other, and she was willing to make the change going all in if that's where I felt God wanted us to be. She just wanted it to be God and not me this time. She knew my heart was to reach out to men helping them to face their struggles, to overcome the same struggles that I had been entangled in most of my life.

We were in agreement that we would change churches, only this time, I was going to do it right. I didn't want to burn any bridges or hurt any feelings. We were in pursuit of God and following the lead of His Holy Spirit.

Right or wrong, I didn't want to close any doors that I may want to walk back through someday. I set up meetings with both pastors, present and future. Telling the one how God was leading us there, our intent to commit and our willingness to serve. While explaining to the other that it was time for us to move on. We had appreciated every opportunity and every moment that we had there. We had reconnected with God there, we had grown so much, and I had found freedom in Jesus. That church received me with open arms with love and acceptance. We would always be grateful for the time spent there.

It was a new year with a new beginning, filled with hope. We had, by no means, arrived anywhere, and while I may still have my struggles, I'm living victorious. There may be weeks that those old thoughts and desires never entered my mind while other times they will flood in. Yes, I am an overcomer, victorious only because of Jesus. I can never accomplish anything in my life without *Him*, and I must always remember that!

It's in those times that we think that "we" can handle something, we're only setting ourselves up for failure!

> No, in all these things we are more than conquerors through him who loved us. (Rom. 8:37, NIV)

I only strive to be in His will, remaining sensitive to the gentle nudging of the Holy Spirit!

That is why we labor and strive, because we have put our hope in the living God, who is the Savior of all people, and especially of those who believe. (1 Tim. 4:10, NIV)

Finally, brothers and sisters, rejoice! Strive for full restoration, encourage one another, be of one mind, live in peace. And the God of love and peace will be with you. (2 Cor. 13:11, NIV)

Make sure that nobody pays back wrong for wrong, but always strive to do what is good for each other and for everyone else. (1 Thessalonians 5:15, NIV)

Conclusion

Now I've never really related to professional sports figures or movie stars. While some may have an incredible testimony of their life, I personally have never been able to connect with them. I admit God has a plan and purpose for each and every one of us, you, me, everyone else and them included.

It's guys like Peter, James, and John who were common everyday fishermen. Jesus knew they had no special skills, still, he called them to follow Him. I'm no Peter, but I've denied Him on multiple occasions. Like Thomas, I have doubts, but I have never put my hand in Jesus's side. I feel that if I had been around in Jesus's day, He very well may have called on me to follow Him.

I've been open and honest about the struggle with life, pornography, and the sexual sin in my life. In and out of church my most of my life. The on again, off again relationship with God. All the ups and downs of life I continued to only sink deeper into spiritual darkness. Each time only took me to a new low.

> ""When an impure spirit comes out of a person, it goes through arid places seeking rest and does not find it." Matthew 12:43 NIV

> "Then it goes and takes with it seven other spirits more wicked than itself, and they go in and live there. And the final condition of that person is worse than the first. That is how it will be with this wicked generation." Matthew 12:45 NIV

After years of denial, I'm owning my faults and transgressions. I am moving from blaming others as an excuse for my actions to take full responsibility for my actions. Me, myself, and I, self-centered, transformed into seeking to be Christ-centered, focused on Him.

It took years before I came to the understanding of how the grip of sin in my life had created deep-seated addictions. More often than not, I would only trade one compulsion for another, sinking further into spiritual darkness.

As I allowed the Holy Spirit to shed light on my addictions those chains truly began to break, it was Jesus who I finally allowed to fill the void in my life. In some ways, it goes beyond even that as we make choices every day, and we always make the final decision. I decided *no more* playing church, no more pretending to be a Christian, no more trying to ride a fence, keeping a foot in both worlds. I chose to become accountable, transparent, and even vulnerable to people in my life. I am going against everything I had come to believe in life. I am exposing every hidden corner of my life to the light of Jesus. No more secrets mean that there is nothing left for Satan to hold over me.

As I began to pray, my heart softened, but that wasn't enough. My mind, the way I thought, my views started to change. We all

CONCLUSION

must continue to allow God to transform us to be more Christ-like. I would dare measure our transformation by; the words we speak, the thoughts that run through our mind and finally what we treasure in our heart.

> Do not conform to the pattern of this world, but be transformed by the renewing of your mind. Then you will be able to test and approve what God's will is— his good, pleasing and perfect will. (Rom. 12:2, NIV)

Maybe you're facing some of the same struggles I have. Then again, perhaps it's something completely different. Whatever type of struggle we are dealing with, it doesn't matter what name we give it up, if it's sin, compulsion or addiction. It all comes in a wide variety of desires. Remember "anything" that you put before God, becomes sin. The one thing I can promise you, you're not facing anything new. There is someone out there that has been where you're at—find that someone, who is willing to disciple you.

OUR STRUGGLES ARE REAL!

"Your struggle is real!"
We face our struggles and overcome our addictions.

> No, in all these things we are more than conquerors through him who loved us. (Romans 8:37, NIV)

We look back at where we've been. We thank God for His grace and mercy. The thought of how "the struggle was real," runs through our mind. Remarkably, we lived through our mess. Our journey has created who we are, giving us compassion for others struggling where we ourselves have been. This is equipping us with the ability to relate as our life is a testimony of hope. We can now reach out to others because we are relatable and help them to also become an overcomer.

It doesn't end there, and every day, we face choices. Just as I believe that we must never forget where we've been, we must always remember who we are. I am a child of God!

As long as we have breath in our body, the war will continue. Praise God. Jesus Christ defeated Satan as His life was sacrificed for

CONCLUSION

us. Then Jesus rose from the grave on the third day, completing the means that we may have eternal life and loving us so much that He allows us to choose who we will serve. A choice that we make every day.

Defeated, Satan continues in his attempt to bring down as many Christians as he possibly can—by whatever means possible that will draw our focus off God, to trip us up, and cause us to fail.

Yes, in some cases, we receive complete and total healing, deliverance, and restoration. Praise God!

Still, there are some things that we have to walk out in faith.

"The struggle is real!"

The End…for now.

#Time for men to step up
#Our Struggles are Real
#IronMen discipleship
#I am a child of God
#God uses men like us to reach other men like us

About the Author

Rick grew up in a small town in Kansas. He knew at an early age God had a calling on his life. He just took the long way to get there. He and Lisa have been married for forty years. He is a father of two and Papa of four. Recently ordained, he is stepping into his calling of evangelism. He started an IronMen discipleship group in 2017. He organized and spoke at an IronMen conference in 2018 and started a second IronMen discipleship group in 2019.

CPSIA information can be obtained
at www.ICGtesting.com
Printed in the USA
BVHW081342030820
585339BV00001B/43